T0355264

The Misadventures of Master Mugwort

A Joke Book Trilogy from Imperial China

The Hsu-Tang Library of Classical Chinese Literature

Made possible by a generous gift from Hsin-Mei Agnes Hsu-Tang 徐心眉 and Oscar L. Tang 唐騮千, the Hsu-Tang Library presents authoritative, eminently readable translations of classical Chinese literature, ranging across three millennia and the entire Sinitic world.

Series Editors
Wiebke Denecke 魏樸和, *Founding Editor-in-Chief*
Lucas Klein 柯夏智, *Associate Editor*

Editorial Board

Cheng Yu-yu 鄭毓瑜
Wilt L. Idema 伊維德
Victor H. Mair 梅維恆
Michael Puett 普鳴
Xi Chuan 西川
Pauline Yu 余寶琳

The Misadventures of Master Mugwort

A Joke Book Trilogy from Imperial China

艾子雜說・艾子後語・艾子外語

Su Shi 蘇軾, Lu Cai 陸采, Tu Benjun 屠本畯

Translated by
Elizabeth Smithrosser

OXFORD
UNIVERSITY PRESS

Oxford University Press is a department of the University of Oxford.
It furthers the University's objective of excellence in research, scholarship,
and education by publishing worldwide. Oxford is a registered trade mark of
Oxford University Press in the UK and in certain other countries.

Published in the United States of America by Oxford University Press
198 Madison Avenue, New York, NY 10016, United States of America.

© Oxford University Press 2023

All rights reserved. No part of this publication may be reproduced, stored in a retrieval system,
or transmitted, in any form or by any means, without the prior permission in writing of Oxford
University Press, or as expressly permitted by law, by license or under terms agreed with the
appropriate reprographics rights organization. Inquiries concerning reproduction outside the
scope of the above should be sent to the Rights Department, Oxford University Press, at the
address above.

You must not circulate this work in any other form and you must impose this same condition
on any acquirer

Library of Congress Cataloging-in-Publication Data
2023915083

ISBN 978-0-19-758560-3

Printed by Sheridan Books, Inc., United States of America.

For Karwin

Contents

Acknowledgments

I will begin by thanking Founding Editor-in-Chief Wiebke Denecke and Associate Editor Lucas Klein for taking on a young scholar with an unusual project. Along the way, I have profited from their wise comments and suggestions as well as those of Stefan Vranka, who has been a steadfast and encouraging guide from start to finish, along with Mengdie Zhao. The advice of the anonymous reviewers also greatly improved the final outcome, especially those of Reader 1, who, despite what must have at times been painful reading, placed criticism in an encouraging voice and pushed me towards a boldness of approach that, I hope, does justice to the original text. My friend and colleague Xiaojing Miao kindly read through the first translation drafts and saved many of my own goals and missed penalties, for which I am inexpressibly thankful. The final translation has also benefitted from Eleanor Goodman's inspired eye and production support from Kathleen Fearn and Dan Gill at OUP. Any remaining mistakes are my own.

Somewhere between cliché and convention in Humor Studies prefaces is a quote by E.B. White, which likens explaining a joke to dissecting a frog: though we may understand its intricacies very well indeed, it is now a dead frog. And now it is my turn. If the metaphor for explaining humor is a violent one, for translating humor it is nothing short of macabre. There, the task of dissection is but a preliminary step towards the end goal of performing a sort of taxidermy, twisting its limp and undignified body until it reassumes a recognizably lifelike state. Translating jokes is grisly work that might have made for a cold-hearted translator, were it not for the enthusiastic warmth that always seems to follow quickly on the heels of the initial bemusement when others hear about the project. Even frog taxidermy has its aficionados, and there seem to be many more who are keen to read humor in translation. I hope the finished product gives them what they are looking for.

The manuscript was completed in the first half of 2022 during my time as a Research Fellow at the International Institute for Asian Studies, in Leiden, the Netherlands. A partial translation was completed during my PhD years, supported by the Clarendon Fund with Pembroke College. I thank my thesis supervisor, Barend ter Haar, as well as Robert Chard and Dirk Meyer, who examined the relevant chapter, and the University of Oxford China Centre Classical Chinese Reading Group. Pi-ching Hsu provided helpful comments at UC Berkeley in 2019, while Rao Xiao and Yanran Li shared some useful resources with me. My family and good friends like Amanda Zhang, Joshua Little, Sooyun Chai, and Xiaochu Wu, among many others, have supported and encouraged me. And then there is Karwin who, as a thoughtful and frank reader, has been privy not just to the eventual frogs but all the botched iterations that preceded them, all the while doing an eminent job of behind-the-scenes taking care of their translator. I hope that he too has found joy in that process, and I dedicate this book to him.

Leiden, November 2022

Dynastic Timeline for Premodern China

Shang (Yin) Dynasty 商 (ca. 1300–1046 BCE)

Zhou Dynasty 周 (ca. 1046–256 BCE)

Western Zhou 西周 (ca. 1046–771 BCE)

Eastern Zhou 東周 (770–256 BCE)

Spring and Autumn Period 春秋 (770–481 BCE)

Warring States Period 戰國 (481–221 BCE)

Qin Dynasty 秦 (221–207 BCE)

Han Dynasty 漢 (206 BCE–220 CE)

Former/Western Han 前漢 / 西漢 (206 BCE–8 CE)

Xin Dynasty 新 (9–23)

Later/Eastern Han 後漢 / 東漢 (25–220)

Wei 魏 Dynasty (220–265) / Three Kingdoms 三國

Jin 晉 Dynasty (265–420)

Western Jin 西晉 (265–316)

Eastern Jin 東晉 (317–420)

Northern and Southern Dynasties 南北朝 (420–589)

Sui Dynasty 隋 (581–618)

Tang Dynasty 唐 (618–907)

Five Dynasties 五代 (907–960)

Song Dynasty 宋 (960–1279)

Northern Song 北宋 (960–1127)

Southern Song 南宋 (1127–1279)

Yuan Dynasty (Mongols) 元 (1271–1368)

Ming Dynasty 明 (1368–1644)

Qing Dynasty (Manchus) 清 (1644–1911)

Names and Dates of the Warring States

Chu 楚	488–223 BCE
Hann 韓	424–230 BCE
Qi 齊	410–221 BCE
Qin 秦	490–221 BCE
Wei 魏 (Liang 梁)	445–225 BCE
Yan 燕	497–222 BCE
Zhao 趙	475–222 BCE

The State of Han is romanized Hann for disambiguation purposes as per convention. Dates from Loewe and Shaughnessy 1999, 28–29. Some of these polities existed prior to the provided start dates, which are based on the accession of certain rulers.

Introduction

Meet Master Mugwort

Readers of any book on Chinese thought and literature will find themselves introduced to multiple "Masters" (*zi* 子) within a matter of pages. Vivid in their diverse personalities, from the irascible Mencius to the capricious Zhuangzi, these early Chinese figures remained enduringly relevant throughout the ensuing dynasties and continue to inspire today. As the protagonists of a corpus of Masters literature, they have been venerated as icons of classical philosophy, with the books that bear their names tapped for wisdom on everything from statecraft and business to parenting and mental health.[1] Over the years, discussion has arisen over the level and manner of contribution made by such figures to the collections of sayings attributed to them. Who was this Master? Was he actually more than one person? And could he really have said that?

This volume introduces readers to yet another "Master": Aizi 艾子 or "Master Ai," here rendered "Master Mugwort."[2] Mugwort's case prompts no such controversies, since he never existed, and therefore could have never uttered the words recorded in the three collections that bear his name. He was not a contemporary of those revered classical thinkers among whom he mingles, but rather an invented character who first appeared over a millennium later, during the Song dynasty (960–1279).

One thing Mugwort does share with his more eminent peers, however, is how his words, actions, and personality remained a source of fascination generation after generation, providing food for thought and inspiring creative engagement in those who encountered him. Over many centuries, the fruits of this engagement took shape as the written tradition contained in this volume, which brings three *Master Mugwort* compilations together in

---

1 See Denecke 2017.

2 Alternatively, "Aicius," or even "Mugwortius." While the Chinese characters used for family names mostly do carry a meaning, by convention these are transliterated rather than translated. In this case, however, it is clear that the family name Ai was no arbitrary choice on the part of the originator; for example, *Ai* may be an intentional homophone of *ai* 騃, or "fool," making him "Master Fool." See "Gaishi zassetsu." Puns based on meanings of family names are a regular feature in premodern Chinese humor compilations, and the author of *Outer Sayings* (hereafter abbreviated OS) clearly had the protagonist's name and its meanings at the forefront of his mind in episodes such as *The Master himself* (OS:15) and *Lordships and lovelies* (OS:22).

English-language translation for the first time. We start at the protagonist's beginnings—at least insofar as they can be traced—with the Song dynasty collection *Miscellaneous Stories of Master Mugwort* (*Aizi zashuo* 艾子雜說). The originator of this work is uncertain, but throughout history it has been attributed to the literary superstar Su Shi 蘇軾 (1037–1101; sobriquet Dongpo 東坡 "East Slope"). The original collection circulated sporadically over the years before experiencing a renaissance during the Ming dynasty (1368–1644). It was amid the print and publishing boom of this period that the enduring popularity of the work kindled at least two entirely new *Mugwort* collections, posturing as sequels—or perhaps encores—to the original. The first was compiled in 1516 by an outrageously talented teenager by the name of Lu Cai 陸采 (1497–1537), who chose for it the title of *Further Sayings of Master Mugwort* (*Aizi houyu* 艾子後語). The second dates itself to 1608, as one of the many retirement projects of the whimsically-minded governor Tu Benjun 屠本畯 (1542–1622), who opted for the slightly more reticent title of *Outer Sayings of Master Mugwort* (*Aizi waiyu* 艾子外語).[3] For young and old, then, the adventures and misadventures of "Master Mugwort" have amused, charmed, and entertained for many centuries. This translation hopes to continue in this vein by introducing this beloved character to a new readership.

The *imaginaire* roamed by Mugwort is a Warring States world as transmitted by the classical canon—the very same world, in fact, as inhabited by many of the better-known Masters. He slips on their guises and acts out their roles: we find him as a minister at the court of the State of Qi, on diplomatic missions at court, or on the road with disciples in tow. We see him serving as regional prefect, and engaging in mock philosophical discussions with others. But we also follow him into more intimate spheres, such as in the role of a teacher instructing his disciples, and we meet his family, blood brothers, neighbors, and goats. Along the way, he encounters famous kings and historical figures, as well as utter nobodies, in episodes that broach both era-defining events and everyday happenings. The collections boast a colorful cast of physiognomists, farmers, and snake charmers and do not shy away from behind-the-scenes political maneuvers, bribery, and intrigue. The free rein the character is given to traverse the time, space, and social spheres of this historical imaginary allows us to explore the extent of the "Warring States world" as conceived in the Song and Ming. These are more

---

3   The contents of some Masters literature, such as *Zhuangzi*, are divided into "inner" and "outer" chapters, the outer chapters sometimes considered a less fundamental part of the text or more dubious in terms of authorship. An alternative translation is "Outer Aphorisms of Master Mugwort/Aicius."

than collections of fictional anecdotes. Rather, they are slideshows of how people in our past imagined their own.

China in the Warring States period

The three *Master Mugwort* collections translated in this volume are set in a portion of early Chinese history known as the Warring States period. This is the name history has chosen for the second part of the Eastern Zhou dynasty, when China consisted of a multistate system under the loosely recognized rule of the Zhou kings.[4] Traditionally starting in 475 BCE, the Warring States period ended in 221 BCE with the conquest of all other states by the westerly State of Qin, whose king, Ying Zheng 嬴政 (whom we shall meet in the *Mugwort* collections), unified the states under centralized governance as the first in what turned out to be a relatively unbroken line of ruling emperors for over two millennia of imperial Chinese history.[5]

Prior to his ascent to emperorship, however, Ying Zheng had been the king of one state among many on the main stage of "All Under Heaven" (*tianxia* 天下), a term used for what was considered the culturally recognizable or civilized world. At the time, this corresponded roughly to the territory of the seven states that will appear most often in the pages of this book. The State of Qin was to the west, covering most of Shaanxi with its capital located close to present-day Xi'an. In a matter of centuries, it would unfold eastwards and annex all other states in its path. In the south, stretching from the bottom of Shaanxi across Hubei and Anhui to Jiangsu province was the vast state of Chu. Along the eastern coast covering most of today's Shandong province was Qi. As the primary base of the character of Master Mugwort, this is the state to which we will pay the most visits over the following pages. Across the Bohai Sea gulf from the neck of the Liaoning peninsula to today's Beijing lay Yan, while its neighbor Zhao's northernmost territory wound along the Yellow River and stretched south to areas of Shanxi and Hebei. Roughly, the outer regions of these states represent the extent of the realm depicted in the *Mugwort* collections. Two further major states, Wei and Hann, occupied the central region, surrounded by other states on all sides. These seven states are usually considered the major players of the period, and the majority of episodes are set in or otherwise involve them. But these seven shared this region with a number

---

4   This account emphasizes those aspects most relevant to the *Master Mugwort* collections. For more on the Warring States period, see Loewe and Shaughnessy 1999, Pines 2009, and Graham 1989.

5   This series follows a timeline of 481 BCE according to the symbolic ending of the *Spring and Autumn Annals* (*Chunqiu* 春秋) after which the period was named. The Warring States period, meanwhile, was named for the Han compilation *Intrigues of the Warring States* (*Zhanguo ce* 戰國策) (Tsien 1993, 1).

Map of the Warring States ca. 350 BCE

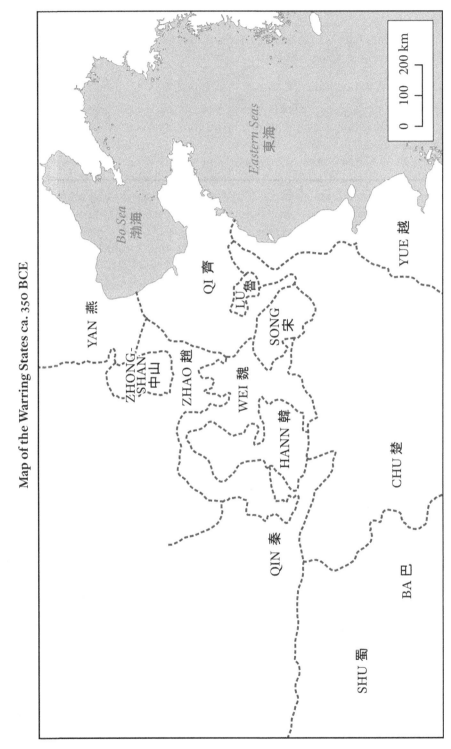

A map of the Warring States, ca. 350 BCE. As implied by the name "Warring States," this was an era of constantly shifting borders and disappearing states. This map is intended merely to supply a rough indication of the locations of the major states we shall encounter in the *Master Mugwort* collections. See Tan 1982.

of smaller and shorter-lived states, as well as fiefdoms and the region that surrounded the largely defunct dynastic capital of the Zhou dynasty.[6] The State of Lu, a once-grand state that had been home to Confucius, features often in the collections as the neighbor of Qi. In the Warring States period it occupied the area around today's Qufu in Shandong. Xue, an area controlled by Qi which its royal house awarded to loyal vassals as a fiefdom, also appears on a regular basis, as does Ju, a city-state within Qi.

Each of the major states had their own capitals and courts, where the ruler, the men in his service, and courtiers of other kinds were based. It was during the Warring States that many of these lineages asserted their regional dominance on the multi-state stage by commandeering the title "king" (*wang* 王). Most of the ruling figures we shall meet in the *Master Mugwort* collections use this title, but we do encounter the occasional "lord" (*gong* 公), or "marquis" (*hou* 侯), which can be understood similarly as holding authority over a given regional jurisdiction. The talents, hobbies, follies, and vices of this array of Warring States kings remained vivid in the minds of Song and Ming readers, having been transmitted not just by texts like the continually popular *Intrigues of the Warring States* (hereafter *Intrigues*), an eclectic collection of episodes mostly set in and around Warring States courts, but also by constituents of the classical canon of Masters literature such as *Mencius*, which relates its titular Warring States master's ethical discussions with these kings.[7]

The name of the period, which was given by later generations, hints at the constant competition that played out among the states among whom All Under Heaven was distributed.[8] The idea of vying for primacy and domination of All Under Heaven was a dream to which only one or two states could ever realistically aspire. Instead, the status quo for the majority of medium, evenly-matched states was more of game of survival, which in

---

6   Many of these smaller states were shorter-lived during the Warring States, but as polities, some had been around since much earlier. The status of the nominal Zhou capital in relation to the other states is complex. The *Mugwort* collections do not concern themselves with the issue; only one episode (OS:21) is set there. Interested readers can refer to Loewe and Shaughnessy 1999, 597–619.

7   Down the ages, the wily figures and artful schemes described in *Intrigues* came to characterize the era for those in later dynasties (Smithrosser 2022). The *Intrigues* were a key textual influence on the *Mugwort* compilations, especially *Outer Sayings*, whose author borrowed its name for the title of the overall collection that houses it. See Appendix 2 and Smithrosser 2021, 147–183.

8   The well-known English translation "Warring States" is something of a misnomer. The Chinese term *zhanguo* is not quite so specific, meaning "fighting" (in a broad sense), or "contending" states. The arena of warfare was certainly one field in which the states vied for security and primacy, but this was not an age of all-out war.

Map of the Warring States Qi ca. 350 BCE

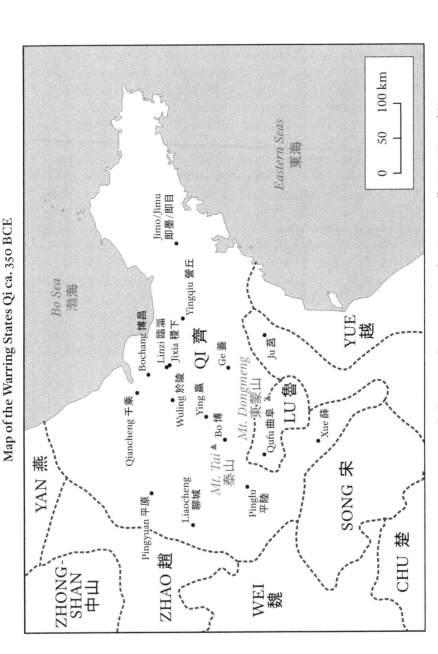

A map of Warring States Qi, ca. 350 BCE, with placenames that appear across the *Mugwort* collections. Xue and Pingyuan were fiefdoms whose lands extended beyond the indicated settlement. Yingqiu is indicated anachronistically. See Tan 1982.

practice meant warfare, diplomatic and marriage alliances, and a working economy. To these ends, rulers and other figures with power quickly developed an awareness of the value of human resources. Know-how
and expertise, be it with regard to diplomacy, battle strategy, or statecraft,
were seen as vital to the fate of a given state in this precarious environment. With travel and communication relatively unhindered, the desire of
different courts to recruit men who could offer useful advice gave rise to
an "interstate market of talent."[9] Thus, beyond territory and resources,
states began to compete for advisors. If a ruler valued the advice or services of a given man, he would attempt to secure his loyalty by granting
a salary, high-level governmental role, title, tax-fief, riches, a princess's
hand in marriage, and so on. Such lavish opportunities did not go unan-
swered: this "market" jostled with a class of intellectuals known as "men
of service" (shi 士). The character of Master Mugwort is represented as
just such a man.

The loyalties of a man of service were not necessarily bound by a state
affiliation akin to the modern concept of nationality. He could grow up
in one state, learn his trade in another, and serve in yet another. Over
the course of his career, he might spend decades in the service of one
monarch before choosing to serve another. Thus a figure like Li Si 李斯
was born and trained in Chu and, seeing no future for the state, went
over to Qin and so impressed its king with his advice that he rose to the
station of Prime Minister. Others did not enjoy such lengthy stints in favor,
and sojourned in states on a short-term basis, bent on obtaining access
to a monarch's ear and then impressing him with ideas and rhetoric to
secure a salaried position. These were the so-called "traveling persuaders"
(youshui zhi shi 遊說之士).[10] Our fictional protagonist, Master Mugwort,
is apparently one of the more successful of his peers. All three collections
open with an episode at the court of Qi, which is presented throughout
as his primary base and the state by which his services are patronized,
though he does regularly appear on the road or in other states for un-
specified reasons.

When a member of this class of intellectual was trusted by his ruler,
particularly when this was due to his skills in rhetoric and persuasion
(see "Persuasions and disputations" below), he might also have been sent
on diplomatic missions to the courts of other states. As a representative,
his role at the other court was to persuade its ruler not to take actions that

---

9   Pines 2009, 3.

10 This is just one of number of variations of the term in Chinese. *Youshi* 遊士 "traveling
    man of service" is also commonly encountered. J.I. Crump in his *Intrigues* translation
    popularized the rendering "wandering persuader" (1996).

might run counter to the interests of his own monarch's state. Being stationed in another state often involved forging and maintaining alliances: a coalition of several smaller states, for example, could counterbalance aggressive actions by a more powerful one, which is another role we see Mugwort fulfill.[11]

With consultancy opportunities on the "interstate market" so attractive and lucrative, it should come as no surprise that many among the younger generation were keen to learn the tools of the trade. This they did by attaching themselves to an established "master," traveling along with him from state to state to learn his rhetorical skills, battle stratagems, and philosophies of statecraft. The master would take on an active pedagogical role, testing his disciples and explaining his processes. Much of the canon of early Chinese thought, familiar both today and when these *Master Mugwort* compilations were written, are ostensibly collections of a given master's remarks or dialogues, recorded and collated by his disciples.[12] The *Mugwort* collections could be considered a lite parody of, or at least modeled around, this genre of Masters literature: Mugwort is constantly spouting pithy remarks and tidbits of wisdom as teaching points, typically with a humorous twist. Sometimes these are explicitly directed at his entourage of disciples, such as "Disciples, take note! Beware of deceiving yourselves!"[13] Others are tacked on at the end, seemingly addressed to nobody in particular. His "disciples" in these cases are none other than ourselves.

Beyond the courts and the master-disciple framework, another Warring States social setup colorfully portrayed in the *Master Mugwort* collections is the "retinue."[14] This was a structure whereby a landed nobleman or figure otherwise of means patronized a cohort of retainers and/or boarded them at his estate for advisory and entertainment purposes. These enfeoffed lords were usually related to the royal bloodline and often held a

---

11 E.g., *King Anxi asks Master Mugwort about Qi* (MS:3). A smaller state aligning itself with a more powerful one (Qin) was known as a "vertical" partnership, while an alliance between smaller states to counterbalance a larger one was known as a "horizontal" one. See Loewe and Shaughnessy 1999, 634. Hence "vertical-horizontalists" (*zonghengjia* 縱橫家) is a common term for specialists in alliance-forging, and was used by extension to all traveling persuaders. In translation it is usually found as "Coalition Advisors" or the "School of Diplomacy."

12 Denecke 2017.

13 From *The five lives of Pingyuan* (OS:19). The "scene of instruction" is one defining feature of Masters literature (Denecke 2011).

14 I have used "retinue" and "retainer" throughout as an approximation for several related Chinese terms. "Entourage" is another common translation.

simultaneous prime ministerial role in government. Mugwort interacts with such historical figures over the course of the three collections, and one episode even mentions that he himself spent three years as part of one.[15] Retinues provided another career option for the aforementioned traveling persuaders. Much like the states themselves, the men at the helm of retinues would compete between themselves to attract and maintain talented retainers. Reportedly, the larger retinues numbered in the thousands. These entities began to take on the trappings of a mini-state, acting with a certain level of autonomy both on the diplomatic stage and the battlefield, as we see for example in *The Lord of Pingyuan's conundrum* (MS:15).

The Warring States period has been continuously held up as one of the most formative ages of premodern China. It was a time of great institutional, intellectual, and social ferment, which paved many of the paths down which Chinese history would unfold. For those in the dynasties that would follow, while always a bygone age unrecognizable compared with their own, it was never a forgotten one. Dialogue-based texts from (or purporting to be from) the Warring States remained ubiquitous in the education system, continuing to be read and memorized, thereby transporting into people's minds a clear image of the environment and zeitgeist in which these thinkers operated along with the thinking itself. Arguably, no other period of early China maintained such a vividly detailed presence in the minds of the literate people of later times. The Warring States world conjured up by the three *Master Mugwort* compilations is just one manifestation of this.

Warring States chronology and the Master Mugwort collections

Warring States period chronology is murky at the best of times, reliant as we are on Han-dynasty writers who were themselves grappling with incomplete records.[16] More recently there have been attempts to reconstruct the historical dates of lives and events as much as the available evidence allows. The process is ongoing, and subject to refinement with ever new archeological finds. When dealing with the *Master Mugwort* compilations, however, their nature as Song and Ming texts raises interesting questions

---

15 *Mr. Jisun's retinue* (FS:3). The most famous retinue-keepers were the "Four Lords" brought together by Sima Qian in *Records of the Historian* (*Shiji* 史記). The Lord of Mengchang, an enfeoffed lord of the Qi royal bloodline and active in the locale, appears most frequently in the *Mugwort* collections.

16 For an outline of the issues of pre-Han chronology with relation to *Records of the Historian*, which has historically been one of the base chronologies, see Nienhauser 1994–, vol. VII, xxvii–xxxii.

as to which schema of dates—premodern or reconstructed—this volume should supply, given that the author-compilers probably had something closer to the *Records of the Historian* chronology in mind. But this is perhaps a moot point, in light of the fact that matters of dating simply do not seem to have been a major concern for the compilers.[17] The titular character, for instance, is endowed with a chronological and spatial fluidity that renders him essentially untrammeled by time and space. Beyond that, there are several examples of interactions between historical Warring States figures that could not have taken place either by traditional or reconstructed chronologies. Given the reduced importance of historicity in dealing with this retrospective Warring States imaginary, this volume does not provide life or reign dates for any pre-Han figures that appear.

Something much more useful than the specific reign dates when reading the *Mugwort* collections is an idea of the sequence of the royal succession lines. The table to the right displays information for those states that appear regularly.[18]

Background to the texts

The *Master Mugwort* collections take the form of an assortment of snapshots from the life of their eponymous protagonist. Eclectic in the scenarios they depict, the episodes do not follow a chronological sequence and vary in length, ranging from a few lines to several pages. Amid this unpredictable cascade of seventy-six encounters, the presence of our esteemed Master is the single constant. The imagined Warring States world through which we accompany him is distant and unfamiliar, yet uncannily recognizable in terms of the bizarre workings of power, society, and human folly. We observe how the Master navigates these, we learn from his aphorisms, guidance, and quips, and are privy to his despair and anger, but above all, bemusement.

Humour is another feature that binds the scenarios together, but the content may not fit neatly into readers' conception of a "joke book." As outlined by Christopher Rea, the term *xiaohua* (笑話, roughly "joke") in modern Chinese, under which similar collections are today anthologized,

---

17 Some might be tempted to put this down to laziness or ignorance, but we must remember that for readers in the know, incongruous interactions like these could well have been a source of humor. Thus they are potentially deliberate. The *Master Mugwort* books are overt in their anachronism, and indeed, wallow in the full range of possibilities it entails. See "Anachronisms" below.

18 After Loewe and Shaughnessy 1999, 28–29, which chiefly follows the reconstructed dates proposed in Yang 1955, 247–272.

Relevant ruling succession lines for frequently appearing states (All BCE)

QI	QIN	WEI (LIANG)	ZHAO	HANN	CHU	YAN
Duke Huan 桓公 (374–357)	King Huiwen 惠文王 (377–311)	Marquis/King Hui 惠侯/王 (369–319)	King Wuling 武靈王 (325–299)	Marquis Zhao 昭侯 (362–333)	King Wei 威王 (339–329)	Kuai, King of Yan 王噲 (320–312)
Marquis/King Wei 威侯/王 (356–320)	King Wu 武王 (310–307)	King Xiang 襄王 (318–296)	King Huiwen 惠文王 (298–266)	King Xuanhui 宣惠王 (332–312)	King Huai 懷王 (328–299)	King Zhao 昭王 (311–279)
King Xuan 宣王 (319–301)	King Zhao 昭王 (306–251)	King Zhao 昭王 (295–277)	King Xiaocheng 孝成王 (265–245)	King Xiang 襄王 (311–296)	King Qingxiang 頃襄王 (298–263)	King Hui 惠王 (278–272)
King Min 湣王 (300–284)	King Xiaowen 孝文王 (250)	King Anxi 安釐王 (276–243)	King Daoxiang 悼襄王 (244–236)	King Xi 釐王 (295–273)	King Xiaolie 孝烈王 (262–238)	King Wuxiao 武孝王 (271–258)
King Xiang 襄王 (283–265)	King Zhuangxiang 莊襄王 (249–247)	King Jingmin 景湣王 (242–228)	Qian, King of Zhao 王遷 (235–228)	King Huanhui 桓惠王 (272–239)	King You 幽王 (237–228)	King Xiao 孝王 (257–255)
Jian, King of Qi 王建 (264–221)	King Zheng 政王 (246–221) (then First Emperor of the Qin dynasty)	Jia, King of Wei 王假 (227–225)	Jia, Stand-in King of Zhao 代王嘉 (227–222)	An, King of Hann 王安 (238–230)	Fuchu, King of Chu 王負芻 (227–223)	Xi, King of Yan 王喜 (254–222)

Names have been edited to match those used in *Miscellaneous Stories*, and titles have been translated rather than transliterated. For the earlier monarchs and any questions regarding these dates, consult Loewe and Shaughnessy 1999, 28–29.

is just as likely to refer to humorous anecdotes than a generic canned gag.[19] Compiled humor in the "anecdotic voice" was typically collected from previous points in history, and the *Mugwort* collections take advantage of this convention to invent historically based scenarios. While they share the fundamental setting, premise, and format, the three collections are products of their own times—the Song and Ming dynasties—two time periods that were themselves separated by half a millennium. Each collection not only reflects the personal touch of the author, but also expresses the concerns of his era; the *Master Mugwort* collections are much less parodies of Warring States matters than they are satires of their own day and age, whereby the Warring States setup is a vehicle through which to poke fun at current affairs and human folly more broadly.[20] The authors of both Ming sequels draw attention to this satirical facet of the tradition in their prefaces and announce their intention to continue in this vein.[21]

Anachronisms

The *Master Mugwort* collections are peppered with anachronisms, ranging from references to material culture and social structures that did not yet exist, to poetic allusions to later texts, to mentions of figures who had not yet been born. The most apparent example is the Buddhist references that pervade this fictional Warring States world. The period ended centuries before Buddhism took root in China. "Chu's Lord of Chunshen was upholding the Five Buddhist Precepts," opens one episode, while the punchline of another hinges on the name of a famous pilgrim-monk from the Tang dynasty (618–907).[22] Indeed, the anachronistic quality of the texts did not go unnoticed in premodern times, and raised the

19 See Rea 2015. The notion of *xiaohua* and "joke" are not perfect synonyms. The rubrics *xiaohua*, "joke," and "jestbook" under which this corpus of texts has been anthologized and studied have obscured how it was conceptualized and discussed on the late-Ming publishing scene (Smithrosser 2021, 63–82). The reader should also note that the definition of "joke" as defined by Humor Studies specialists is much more specific than the day-to-day usage of the term (Attardo 2014, 417–418).

20 While this translation does point out some instances of satire, it leaves the task of comprehensive interpretation to future scholarship.

21 The prefaces are translated in *Further Sayings* and Appendix 2. This emphasis draws our attention to the didactic quality with which Chinese humor was theoretically bound (Xu 2011). On account of this facet, the collections have also been regularly anthologized as "fables" (*yuyan* 寓言) in modern times. More literally translated as "lodged words," this term refers to text that employs an analogous scenario to express a message. On this facet of Chinese humor, see Lin 2006.

22 *The Lord of Chunshen's elderly ox* (OS:14), and *Master Mugwort's disciples stage an intervention* (MS:5), respectively.

eyebrows of figures such as one premodern commentator who remarked of *Miscellaneous Stories*, "This book, for its part, contains many events from later ages."[23]

Some readers might find this anachronistic quality jarring, and it is certainly one of the reasons the texts have occasionally been treated with disdain in existing scholarship, which presumes that these anachronisms are careless slips or historical ignorance on the part of the writers. But we should remember that these jarring incongruities, which appear at irregular intervals and have the effect of bizarrely interrupting the Warring States pretense of the text, can also act as a great source of amusement. I would contend that a majority of these were deliberately—even judiciously— inserted for their readers' entertainment.

Persuasions and disputations

One of the defining features of the Warring States period were the methods of rhetoric used in speeches to gain the agreement of a ruler. One broad term for this was "explanation" (*shui/shuo* 說), often rendered "persuasion" on account of its usual function as a speech intended to persuade a ruler to adopt or reject a given proposal.[24] The form has its conventions: the heavy use of analogies to help the ruler grasp the issue in the manner desired, with questions asked along the way to make sure he was keeping up to speed. If at the end the ruler found himself sufficiently persuaded, he would typically say something like "Good!" (*shan* 善), to indicate his approval, or order the suggested plan of action be put in motion there and then. This formula was immortalized by the *Intrigues* and Masters literature, and will become familiar over the coming pages. Rulers would invite men of service to court in anticipation of hearing their consult in the form of a "persuasion." In *The King of Yan's predicament* (MS:24), for example, Mugwort makes a cryptic remark that prompts the King of Yan to request, "Do elaborate with a persuasion."[25] A talented, unemployed persuader would actively seek out opportunities to speak to the monarch and wow his way into a job using persuasions, as in *Fan Sui is granted an audience with King Zhao* (MS:19) and *Master Mugwort asks Chunyu Kun about Zou Ji* (MS:27). A third party, be that a state or a private individual, could also implore or bribe a skilled persuader to argue their case with the ruler, a scenario we see play out time and time again across the *Master Mugwort* collections.

---

23 Chen 1936, 69.
24 The "scene of persuasion" is a defining feature of Masters literature (Denecke 2011).
25 Literally, "Do you have a persuasion for that?"

Another Warring States type of argumentation we shall encounter, though less for the purposes of government, is "disputation" (*bian* 辩).[26] This often took the form of a hyper-logical dissection of concepts that ended with the listener conceding something completely illogical. In court settings, disputation may have had an element of performance or entertainment.[27] The originator of *Miscellaneous Stories*, at least, seems to have viewed such discussions with much bemusement, often riffing on the theme to show us failed attempts, for example in *Master Mugwort is challenged to a logical duel* (MS:17), in which a dense yet self-assured intellectual makes a cringeworthy and drawn-out attempt to distill a universal logical rule to explain the presence of bells on camels, Buddhist pagodas, hunting birds, and in funeral processions. There is, of course, no such rule; all his hapless endeavor earns him is a sarcastic jab from an exasperated Mugwort.

The Humorists paradigm

One of the most frequently appearing tropes of the *Master Mugwort* episodes is a method of persuasive rhetoric that we shall call the "Humorists paradigm." The textual source of the paradigm is the "Biographies of the Humorists" chapter of *Records of the Historian*.[28] The chapter covers several figures, including the Qi courtier Chunyu Kun who appears frequently in *Master Mugwort* episodes. Each biography demonstrates how a courtier's indirect silly remark or comically exaggerated enthusiasm for a policy can lead an obstinate ruler to realize his own wrongdoing, a method particularly useful when direct remonstration proved ineffective or was forbidden on pain of death. The chapter was extremely well-referenced in the publishing environment in which *Miscellaneous Stories* circulated and the Ming *Master Mugwort*s were composed; publishers regularly invoked the chapter to defend humorous content by underscoring the fact that Sima Qian had asserted its value in a field so sacred as the minister-ruler relationship.[29] Certainly, the paradigm seems to have been a familiar one by the Ming dynasty, with some compilations even collecting anecdotic instances with the explicit aim of teaching readers this specific rhetorical skill.[30] Many episodes see Master Mugwort perform a model

---

26 "Distinction-drawing," (Fraser 2020) and "arguing out alternatives" (Graham 1989) are other renderings that aim to highlight the specific method.

27 Harbsmeier 1998, 301.

28 "Guji/Huaji liezhuan" 滑稽列傳. The correct pronunciation is under debate, see for example Pokora 1972. For a complete translation and discussion of the chapter, see Nienhauser 1994–, vol. XI, 149–195.

29 Smithrosser 2021, 110–116.

30 Smithrosser 2021, 89–92, 112–113.

example of the Humorists paradigm to indirectly remonstrate with a ruling figure (e.g., *Three feet of rope* [FS:1]) and as the sequels progress, it is clear that in the internal world of the text, just as in the world outside of it, the fame of the character's prowess in regard to this particular art is on the rise; several episodes portray other characters seeking Mugwort out to ask for his help. Other episodes play with the paradigm itself, flipping it on its head to show a ruler using it on the persuader, or transplanting it into a domestic setting.[31]

Introduction to the texts

Miscellaneous Stories of Master Mugwort

ATTRIBUTED AUTHOR

The authorship of the original *Master Mugwort* has traditionally been attributed to the Song dynasty literatus Su Shi.[32] He was born in 1037 in Meishan in today's Sichuan province to father Su Xun 蘇洵 (1009–1066), an important literary figure in his own right. In 1057, together with his talented younger brother Su Che 蘇轍 (1039–1112), Su Shi went to the Northern Song capital Kaifeng to take the prestigious "presented scholar" civil service examinations (*jinshi* 進士).[33] Both passed with flying colors and left a deep impression on some of the most important literati of the day. Thus Su Shi's career trajectory, marked as it was by the extremity of its highs and lows, began as it would continue. Su Shi went on to hold a series of regional governorships around the country, such as of the vibrant city of Hangzhou in 1071.[34] Su Shi's writings were widely circulated and well-read in his own day, with fans among the literati, Buddhist monks, and the imperial family alike. The high regard and influence that came hand-in-hand with his talents were always recognized—if not always welcomed—by members of the political scene at the capital. A public-oriented and vocal figure, he composed barbed satirical and remonstrative essays and eventually fell foul of powerful figures at court, as we shall see below in "The Northern Song political context." Narrowly avoiding a death sentence, he was sent into exile, which in actual terms meant being stationed at far-flung, undesirable locations of the empire. His first stint in exile came in 1079, to Huangzhou

---

31 For the former, *Gongsun Long meets his match* (MS:16), for the latter *Master Mugwort's grandson* (FS:6).

32 For a general overview, see Franke 1976, vol. III, 900–968. On the life trajectory of Su Shi with particular reference to his writings, see Egan 1994. For a bibliography of his works and further readings, see Ridgway and Tomlonovic 2017.

33 For respective biographies, see Franke 1976, vols. I–II, 885–900; vol. II, 882–885.

34 And again in 1089.

in modern-day Hubei province. After being recalled, he was exiled again in 1094 to modern-day Guangdong and soon thereafter across the waters to Danzhou on the southerly island of Hainan. This was, in essence, as far as it was possible to send him and a hotbed of tropical disease to boot. Proponents of Su Shi's authorship of *Miscellaneous Stories* believe the work to have been compiled at this point in his life. He died in 1101, mere months after his exoneration when yet another regime change brought him back to the mainland.

Su Shi was a dazzlingly prolific writer in many genres, from poetry and literary prose to governance discourses and memorials to the throne. His writing has come to be known, amongst many things, as the epitome of the "heroic abandon" (*haofang* 豪放) style, and during his lifetime he raised a number of protégés who went on to become significant writers in their own right, such as Huang Tingjian 黃庭堅 (1045–1105).[35] Writing aside, Su Shi was also endowed with a mind-boggling array of other talents and achievements, from painting and calligraphy to gastronomical inventions.

While the humor in Su Shi's writing has been appreciated for almost a millennium, it is a lesser-explored facet of his writing in the academic literature. English-language scholarship has looked at the social uses of playfulness in his poetry while more recent work has spotlighted the role of humor in his interactions with Buddhism.[36] Humor continued to be key in how he was imagined and reinvented as the centuries passed, and in the late Ming, a "Dongpo vogue" in the publishing world spurred on appearances of Su as a character in Ming humor publications and sparked new forms of humor based on his writings.[37] The two *Master Mugwort* sequels translated in this volume are but one manifestation of this phenomenon.

THE ATTRIBUTION DEBATE

The matter of Su Shi's authorship of the original *Master Mugwort* is not a settled one. The long-standing debate over whether *Miscellaneous Stories* rightfully belongs in Su Shi's collected works has had ardent proponents on both sides, and usually stems from doubt over whether this bawdy and "uncouth" (*li* 俚) humorous work could actually have been written by an author so highly revered as Su Shi. Thus, the authorship debate is just as much a story of the winding ways in which Su's vast body of surviving writings has been perceived, assigned internal levels of significance, and

---

35 Yang 2014.
36 On playfulness, see Egan 1994. For Buddhism, see Rao 2019.
37 Smithrosser 2021.

characterized down the ages; and of how the shifting landscape of values and norms in readers' worlds in the meantime, especially with regard to the perceived acceptability of certain kinds of writing, has been invoked to opposite conclusions. The one certainty is that the available evidence does not permit a conclusive verdict for either camp, and today, any movement in either direction seems unlikely unless fresh textual material, or perhaps new digital methods, come to light. Appendix 1 provides an overview of the debate.

What is more important in approaching these translations than Su Shi's actual level of input is the strong association with him that these texts carried for their premodern readers. This is especially true for the Ming collections, which seem to have been composed in the firm belief that they were writing a sequel to a work by Su Shi himself. The current status quo in anthologies is to apply caveats like "previously inscribed as by" (*jiuti* 舊題) or "passed down as by" (*chuan* 傳), which hint at the uncertainty while acknowledging the association with Su Shi held by the work in premodern times.

THE NORTHERN SONG POLITICAL CONTEXT

Regardless of the true identity of the author(s), most agree that the transmitted *Miscellaneous Stories* is a Song text. Certainly, the character of Mugwort was documented during the early Southern Song at the very latest, by figures whose lives crossed the Northern–Southern Song transition, like Zhou Zizhi 周紫芝 (1082–1155).[38] Our protagonist and his satirical quality, at least, does seem to be a Northern Song creation. Perhaps more importantly, the work has been repeatedly read as a satire of Northern Song politics right from the earliest mentions until the present day. Before proceeding to the translation, a brief overview of the relevant issues in the politics of the times is in order, with reference to Su Shi's troubled relationship with them.

The Northern Song, known to history by this name that hints at the catastrophic and traumatic loss of the northern part of its territory following invasion by the Jurchen Jin in 1126–1127, had from its founding in 960 been under threat from powerful states to the north. Peaceful relations were partly maintained by means of frequent payments of goods to the Khitan Liao (916–1125), a vast empire that stretched across the North China Plain, Northeast China, Southern Dauria, the Mongolian Plateau,

---

38 See the poem "I read *Master Mugwort* at night and inscribed this at the end" ("Ye du Aizi shu qiwei" 夜讀艾子書其尾), translated in Smithrosser 2021, 139; quoted in Kong Fanli 1985, 39. For the Ming, see Lu Cai's preface to *Further Sayings*, translated in this volume. For a recent discussion, see Zhou Jin 2017, 39–40.

and part of the Korean peninsula. It is not for nothing that Mugwort's "home state" is Qi, a major state in that it had once posed a challenge for All Under Heaven, rather than the formidable Qin, the eventual victor.[39] While it benefited from its eastern geographical position, a series of less-than-ideal kings and bad governance failed to take advantage of this, and in the end it befell the same fate as all the other states to be gobbled up by Qin. Given that readers were all aware of the historical endgame, the constant descriptions of the follies of Qi governance may carry some sort of warning for the Song in this regard, especially since the Qin threat is made palpable throughout.

While the times in which Su Shi lived were overall an age of peace, his career played out against a tumultuous political backdrop of factional strife. With the empire partly dependent on payments to the Liao, any domestic fiscal pressures had an existential facet to them. A well-functioning state was thus of paramount importance, and there had been regular attempts at reform to that end since the beginnings of the Song. Yet the advent of the reformist Prime Minister Wang Anshi 王安石 (1021–1186) marked a watershed point. History has not been kind to Wang. The many barbed jabs at prime minister figures in *Miscellaneous Stories*, if they were indeed aimed at Wang as has traditionally been understood, are just one example of a large body of critical writings produced by his opponents and their self-appointed moral successors down the ages.[40]

Wang Anshi's rise to power in 1069 marked the beginning of the "New Policies" (*Xinfa* 新法) reforms.[41] Wang's vision for governance was ambitious and all-encompassing, reaching far across the empire and into all types of governance at every level. Monetary and fiscal institutions across the board were replaced with new systems, most of which reduced private control, such as governmental loans for farmers issued by local granaries. The labor and military corvée systems were completely overhauled while local horse-breeding schemes were put in place to ensure a strong cavalry. Water management and irrigation control became a huge state priority, and the civil service examination system was revamped to become more skills-based, while a new set of interpretations and commentaries of the

---

39 On Qi, see Loewe and Shaughnessy 1999, 635–638. While FS:3 does see Master Mugwort "returning" (*fan* 反) to the neighboring polity of Lu, such wording is not definitive.

40 Smithrosser 2016. Lin Yutang (1947) carried this sentiment into modern times.

41 The reform period is also known as the time of "policy changing" (*bianfa* 變法).

classics was introduced.[42] A system of academies was established so the government could take a more direct hand in training the next generation of civil servants. All this meant that the Song empire underwent a sudden and overwhelming amount of change in less than a decade. At least in the timeframe in which the initial reforms were tested out, many could be criticized as short-sighted, overambitious, or unpragmatic. Others were inflexible in the face of regional differences or the year-to-year variations in natural and climatic phenomena. All faced some level of resistance on the ground by those local governors—among them Su Shi—who were tasked with their implementation and did so either half-heartedly or with a great deal of reluctance. *Miscellaneous Stories* frequently takes us to this grassroots level to explore the effects of ill-fitting and inflexible top-down policy-making on the populace and governor figures. Often, the ostensible concern over the New Policies was less about their intentions or goals, and more about their approach and timing. Thus a particular concern with the matter of priorities, especially the folly of misplaced ones, pervades the content of *Miscellaneous Stories*. Even when not placed strictly into a governance context, the scenarios are often conceptually analogous to issues of policy and decision-making.

Throughout history and historiography, Wang's reforms have been synonymous with the fierce resistance from factions who opposed them from a variety of practical and moral standpoints. The changes to the examinations topics and schooling system, as well as the expansion of state money-lending, land distribution, and local household organization in particular stood to diminish the privileged access to higher social status that families of scholar-officials and other courtiers had accrued over generations. Many of these were extremely influential and powerful figures. To be sure, Wang found ways both to stifle dissent and divert the barrage of voices from the ears of the emperor. He blocked pre-existing routes for alternative ideas to impact policy by setting up a new autonomous governmental organ, staffed by trusted figures/cronies to control fiscal matters. Thus the issue of dissent and remonstration, especially with reference to their successful articulation and how figures of power respond thereto, looms large in *Miscellaneous Stories*, seen through the Warring States persuader role of Mugwort, the Humorists paradigm, and in other ways.

One could argue that a more insidious problem than the nature of the policies of either side was the fact that Wang's reforms marked the

---

42 There exist several premodern jokes about Wang Anshi's obsession with water management (see Smithrosser 2016). At least, he does not seem to be censured directly on this in *Miscellaneous Stories*, unless under the rubric of misplaced priorities and a lack of pragmatism.

beginning of over a century of yo-yo politics and disruptive policy reversals that ultimately weakened the dynasty. These U-turns were intimately
tied to the stance of the throne on the issues; after all, it was supposedly
the emperor who wielded ultimate executive power. The primary ena-
bler of Wang Anshi's reforms had been the youthful Emperor Shenzong
(r. 1067–1085), who was ambitious and idealistic and placed his whole
faith, not to mention the full brunt of state resources, at the disposal
of Wang's elaborate vision of statecraft.[43] *Miscellaneous Stories* expresses ample disdain for the harm caused by the extravagant plans of a
well-meaning yet overly idealistic ruler. These proved tumultuous times
for Su Shi, who lambasted, mocked, and remonstrated against several
aspects of the reforms. Widely read in his own day, Su became a thorn
in the side of the regime. By 1079, it could tolerate him no more, and the
famous "Crow Terrace Poetry Trial" (*Wutai shi'an* 烏臺詩案) saw Su Shi
prosecuted and potentially subversive and traitorous interpretations of
his writings quoted in court as evidence against him.[44] After Shenzong
died, however, the throne passed to the sickly child-emperor Zhezong
(r. 1085–1100), and anti-reform figures were recalled to court. Su Shi,
for example, was called back into the limelight and awarded a number
of prestigious roles. Their policy reversals were unrolled far and wide,
as per the preference of his regents. But when his mother died in 1093,
the sixteen-year-old Zhezong moved to reinstate the reformist stance
of his father. Zhezong was constantly ill, however, and after years of
regency he did not enjoy the robust position at court that his father
had. With Wang Anshi now dead, and in the absence of a similarly capable figure to continue his grand vision, the reforms were rolled out
in a compromised and patchy manner, and vicious factional intrigue
ensued. The elderly Su Shi now found himself exiled to the ends of the
empire, beyond even the remit of the former Warring States, only to be
recalled after Zhezong's death in 1100, which precipitated yet another
switch-up in court culture. Thus, another theme in *Miscellaneous Stories* is the dynamic between rulers and their ministers, as well as that
between fathers and sons, a common metaphor in Chinese literature
for rulers and ministers.[45] How the model persuader Mugwort reacts
to and counteracts the Warring States kings' ill-advised ideas, and how
untalented or misguided rulers and ministers are shown to blindly follow

43 Wang Anshi's ideas had earlier been rejected under the previous Emperor Renzong
    (r. 1022–1067), which further illustrates the connection between the ruler's opinion
    and policy stability.
44 Hartman 1990; Lin Yutang 1947, 166–207.
45 Lu Cai explicitly cites this aspect in his preface to *Further Sayings*. See pages 58–59.

others to the detriment of their populace, for example, are scenarios that recur throughout the compilation.

The translation below has not attempted to point out every possible instance of governmental satire or all the likely hints at the Wang Anshi reforms.[46] Moreover, to pin down a connection by firmly dictating the target would do an injustice to this text, seeing as the author deliberately avoided doing so. Part of the beauty of this work, and of the indirectness of satire in general, is that its vagueness endows it with a timeless quality. The Prime Minister butt in *Miscellaneous Stories*, who by extension could stand for any decision-making figure in government, is something that crosses different time contexts. It clearly resonated with people in the Ming, and works just as well in our own times. Thus I am inclined to frame the text as inspired by Wang Anshi, his policies, and those that followed in his footsteps, rather than being about them in a restrictive sense. A work of satire, if intended to have a real-life impact on people's thinking in anything beyond its immediate context, often makes itself broadly applicable in this way.[47] Whoever the author was, I believe this was one of their intentions, and I hope to preserve this aspect in the translation. While I have drawn occasional links as part of the guided reading approach, the majority of stones have been left to be turned by future scholars.

The Ming sequels

MUGWORT IN THE MING

The two Ming *Master Mugwort* compilations were created and circulated in a very different environment than the original. The Yuan and the first half of the Ming saw new imprints of *Miscellaneous Stories*, and with the onset of a print and publishing boom that started to gain ground in the Jiajing reign period (1521–1567), individual *Master Mugwort* episodes began to be picked out and recycled into other books.[48] But the clearest testaments to the popularity (and marketability) of *Miscellaneous Stories* and its central character during the Ming dynasty are the two original sequels translated in this volume. Composed over four hundred years after *Miscellaneous Stories* and close to a century apart from each other (with prefaces dated 1516 and 1608 respectively), these represent a creative engagement with not just the original text, but a protagonist

---

46 One complicating factor is that if the author indeed was Su Shi, his appraisal of Wang Anshi was nuanced, not a blanket rejection. The episodes would need to be examined with the views he expressed towards individual particular policies.

47 After all, this is also why the author has chosen to simulate events in a bygone age.

48 Including those surveyed in Smithrosser 2021, 83–88.

that was emerging as a literary tradition in his own right. Through the inherited framework of the character that had been established by the original, Lu Cai and Tu Benjun likewise used the Warring States world that existed in the minds of their readers as a playground for humor and intertextual twists, this time with their satirical lense set clearly on the concerns of their own day in the Ming. Yet both authors bring to the setup their own distinctive flair. Lu Cai's *Further Sayings* is a somewhat shorter collection of fifteen episodes which deals mostly with everyday issues. Tu Benjun's *Outer Sayings*, on the other hand, with its winding, and at times long-winded, tales of governmental corruption, bureaucratic folly, and social mix-ups, at more than 6500 characters is longer than the original itself, despite having only around half the number of episodes.

The Ming success of *Miscellaneous Stories* and the rise of these sequels must be understood in the context of the wider phenomenon of a "Dongpo vogue," which climaxed at this time, spurred on by the publishing boom.[49] Regardless of the authenticity concerns that surround *Miscellaneous Stories* in modern scholarship, we must remember that these authors believed that they were compiling a sequel to a Su Shi work. In the Ming, that Su Shi had authored the original *Master Mugwort* appears to have been widely accepted as fact. In a move that might seem bold today, Lu Cai opens his preface with "The whole world knows *Master Mugwort* to be the Slope Codger's playful brushstrokes," while Tu Benjun straightforwardly attributes the work to "Gentleman Su the Elder" (Su zhanggong 蘇長公).[50] The only known doubter in the Ming was Hu Yinglin 胡應麟 (1551–1602), who writes, "Due to Su Shi being given to humor and jibes in general, works of this variety are attributed to him one after the other. During the Song, people appraised the Slope on account of the eloquence present in both his joyous laughs and his angry curses. Could his brush really have produced a book this shallow and uncouth?"[51] Indeed as Hu describes, the association was being sustained, propelled and perpetuated by those who republished it. Both in deciding to print *Miscellaneous Stories* and emphasizing the attribution, publishers must have understood how sales benefited from the raging popularity of Su Shi.

---

49 Smithrosser 2021, 184–216.

50 "The Slope," and "Slope Codger" below refer to Su Shi's sobriquet, "East Slope." For Tu's attribution, see the preface in *Further Sayings* and in Appendix 2.

51 Quoted in Zhou Jin 2017, 2. For the original, see Hu Yinglin 1933, 73. Cf. Li Ye 李冶 (1192–1279) of the Yuan dynasty, who in a book with similar purposes to that of Hu Yinglin, believed it to be of "the Slope's hand" (Poshou 坡手) *despite* being "uncouth and vulgar" (*lisu* 俚俗) (Li Ye 1935, 140). Also quoted in Zhou Jin 2017, 2.

The celebration of his "joyous laughs" long outlasted the Song, and was in fact an inextricable facet of how Su Shi was imagined by Ming readers. Su was unambiguously the most featured character in anecdotic humor compilations, while attributed humorous writings were continually published and republished.[52] The connection with Su Shi must have seemed extremely plausible in the contemporaneous context; in expressing his doubt Hu was swimming against the current to the point of idiosyncrasy. The popularity of Su Shi amid the publishing boom was a self-perpetuating feedback loop, churning out new texts that generated more demand and inspired new publications. Before long Su Shi had become the very standard for celebrity, with popular writers finding themselves labeled "even as famous as East Slope."[53] At the height of the Dongpo vogue, the hunger for more Su Shi material outstripped even the prolific corpus he had produced in his lifetime; the impetus to attribute *Miscellaneous Stories* to Su Shi spoke for itself.[54]

As a gift from the publishing conventions and temporal proximity of the Ming, we are fortunate to have prefaces from both the *Further Sayings* and *Outer Sayings* author-compilers that outline their motivations for producing the work and their thoughts on the original.[55] Both Lu Cai and Tu Benjun intended their own offering to be physically appended after the pre-existing *Mugwort* collections.[56] Tu Benjun's compiling strategy was particularly elaborate, pairing the three *Mugworts* (the third his own) with another two texts to create *Jest Intrigues of the Five Masters* (*Wuzi xiece* 五子諧策), a title he consciously picked to channel the spirit of the *Intrigues of the Warring States*.[57] This work is discussed in more detail below.

---

52 Smithrosser 2021, 187–193.

53 Greenbaum 2007, 203.

54 Lest our focus on *Miscellaneous Stories* lead us to lose perspective on the wider issue, it should be said that this is in fact one of the more plausible of the disputed Ming attributions. For a case study of another, see Smithrosser 2021, 194ff.

55 The two men are best understood as "author-compilers." While it is evident that there is a large level of direct authorship involved in both sequels, it would also appear that some content was partially recycled into the collection after being heard or read elsewhere, as is made particularly plain in Lu Cai's preface. The word *zhuan* 撰, one of the most common ways to make an attribution on Ming imprints, is an umbrella term that could indicate an authorial or compiling function.

56 Though Lu Cai's *Further Sayings* did go on to be compiled and published elsewhere in the absence of the original.

57 See Appendix 2 for the preface, and Smithrosser 2021, 161 for a discussion.

FURTHER SAYINGS OF MASTER MUGWORT

While the authorship of *Miscellaneous Stories* remains fraught with doubt, the identity of the men behind *Further Sayings* and *Outer Sayings* is no mystery. The author-compiler of *Further Sayings* was Lu Cai, who was native to Changzhou 長洲 (present-day Suzhou).[58] His original given name had been Zhuo 灼, which he changed to "Cai" later in life. While the *Further Sayings* preface is signed "Lu Zhuo" and premodern and modern editions alike have tended to anthologize the compilation under that name, this volume employs Cai in order to preserve the connection with scholarship on his other literary contributions, which have thus far attracted much more attention.

Much of what we know of Lu Cai comes from the writing of an elder brother Lu Can 陸粲 (1494–1551), who passed the civil service examinations to lead a high-level bureaucratic career and wrote a moving grave inscription for Cai upon his much earlier passing.[59] Lu Cai did not enjoy comparable success on the examination track, reportedly struggling with the required discipline and conformist nature of the process. After several failed attempts, he lost faith in the whole endeavor and threw himself into a life of nonstop drinking, socializing, and play-watching. Before long, however, the world of theater began to repay him with opportunities and he gave up on the exams completely to live off his brush in a different way. Lu Cai's forthright personality, disdain for social expectations, and spontaneous, uninhibited lifestyle come through vividly both in texts that mention him and those of his own hand. He led somewhat of an itinerant life, traveling far and wide across the Ming empire to visit friends. *Further Sayings* was compiled at an inn in Jinling 金陵 (present-day Nanjing), and his travels are amply documented in his description of a trip to Mount Tai as well as the collections of assorted poetry, diary notes, and commemorative pieces from between 1532 and 1534.[60] He died in 1537, characteristically on the road, at around forty years of age.

Today, Lu Cai is remembered most predominantly as a playwright, who composed mostly southern plays (*chuanqi* 傳奇). Not all those known have

---

58 Lu's courtesy name was Zixuan 子玄 and his sobriquet "Mountain-Man of the Heavenly Pool" (Tianchi shanren 天池山人) (*Mingren zhuanji* 1978, 566). "Mountain-man" was a common sobriquet suffix in the Ming, typically used as a self-identifier for those who idealized a reclusive life of unconstrained freedom.

59 See *Mingren zhuanji* 1978, 567–570 and Lu Cai 1974, *juan* 3, 10–11. See also the preface to Lu Cai's poetry collection by Feng Mengzhen 馮夢禎 (1548–1606). When Lu died he left behind a two-year-old son, for whom Feng prepared this preface in 1598. It states that a great many of Lu's writings had already been lost by this time, but also lists some further plays that have disappeared since (Feng Mengzhen, 75–78).

60 Lu Cai 1995–1997, 1–334.

survived, but among those that have, *Record of the Bright Pearl* (*Mingzhu ji* 明珠記) is best-known. Cai completed this forty-three-act play at the precocious age of eighteen in collaboration with his brother.[61] Loosely based on *Wushuang the Peerless* (*Wushuang zhuan* 無雙傳), a Tang marvel tale by Xue Diao 薛調 (ca. 829–872), it was watched and discussed by many of the prominent playwrights of the times to mixed reviews.[62] Other extant plays include a version of *The Western Chamber* (*Xixiang ji* 西廂記) and *The Stolen Incense* (*Huaixiang ji* 懷香記).[63] Beyond drama and the collections listed above, there survives a collection edited by Lu of the writings of painting connoisseur and fellow Suzhou man and travel-lover, Du Mu 都穆 (1459–1525), of whom Lu Cai professes himself a "disciple" (*menren* 門人).[64]

Further Sayings, which carries a preface dated 1516 (Zhengde 11), is one of Lu Cai's earliest surviving works, composed around the age of nineteen with his entire career ahead of him. His self-written preface brusquely recounts how the first known sequel to the original *Master Mugwort* was put together by the bored teenager while away from home with nothing else to do, before announcing his intentions to have it appended after "the one by the Slope Codger." At roughly half the length of the other two, *Further Sayings* is the shortest of the *Master Mugwort* compilations.

OUTER SAYINGS OF MASTER MUGWORT

The final *Master Mugwort* compilation in this volume comes from the self-described "playful brush" (*xibi* 戲筆) of Tu Benjun, courtesy name Tianshu 田叔, also Binsou 闟叟, who was native to the area southeast of

---

61 Though there are differing accounts of extent of this input (Zhang Shuying 2000, 2).

62 See Zhang Shuying 2000, 1–3. For a translation of *Wushuang the Peerless* accompanied by the original Chinese, see Wang Jing 2020.

63 The former, in thirty-six acts, is sometimes found under the title *Heavenly Pool Lu's "Record of the Western Chamber"* (*Lu Tianchi Xixiang ji* 陸天池西廂記). The latter, in twenty-five acts, is a retelling of a story in *New Account of Tales of the World* (*Shishuo xinyu* 世說新語), whereby a father uncovers his daughter's affair when he happens to smell his precious household incense on a beautiful young man. For the former play, with a preface by Lu himself, see *Guben xiqu congkan chuji*, vol. 13. For the latter play, see vol. 14.

64 See Du Mu 1995–1997, 641. Whenever the term "disciple" appears (whether understood in a physical or spiritual sense) it is tempting to imagine a connection with the *Master Mugwort* content. However, from what is known about Lu Cai's early life, *Further Sayings* most likely predates any extensive master-disciple relationship with Du Mu. *Further Sayings* was prefaced in 1516 when Lu Cai was nineteen, and Du Mu died in 1525 when Lu Cai was around twenty-eight.

present-day Ningbo in Fujian province.[65] He was born into an illustrious cluster of Tus, who by Benjun's time had built up a family pedigree of governmental success for generations. His paternal great-great-uncle Tu Yong 屠滽 (1440–1512) had risen to such heights in the official bureaucracy as Minister for Personnel (*Libu shangshu* 吏部尚書), and more immediately, his father Tu Dashan 屠大山 (1500–1579) had served in a number of significant governing roles before his failure to put down coastal pirates saw him stripped of his rank and demoted to "commoner" (*min* 民) status.[66] The only son amid five daughters, Benjun was able to sidestep the cutthroat Ming civil service examination track under the auspices of his father and took up a comfortable position. He held a number of posts over the years, including Prefect of Chenzhou 辰州 (present-day western Hunan) and Salt Distribution Commissioner for Fujian (*yanyun si* 鹽運司). In 1601 he took retirement and returned to his native region with over two decades of life in front of him.

Tu Benjun had always pursued a number of writing projects alongside his official duties, but upon retirement there was an unmistakable uptick in productivity. In his own words, "I did not venture to wile away my days in idleness and so composed this."[67] His overall corpus of surviving works lean towards shorter pieces of encyclopedic nature that gathered information on a particular topic into one place. In recent times, his gastronomical writings have garnered the most scholarly attention. One of his largest works is *Explanatory Notes on Seafood Varieties along the Southeastern Coast* (*Minzhong haicuo shu* 閩中海錯疏), a three-fascicle dictionary prefaced 1596.[68] Another well-studied contribution is *Book-satchel of Tea-leaves* (*Mingji* 茗笈), which collates a variety of texts on the subject of tea, and is included in *The Mountain-Forest Administrator's Companion* (*Shanlin jingji ji* 山林經濟籍).[69]

---

65 As with many Ming writers, existing texts use a number of character variants and homophonic characters for these names, and there are several further self-appellations in circulation. The two names provided are the most commonly encountered. Existing literature tends to take Binsou as a courtesy name (*zi*), rather than a sobriquet (*hao*).

66 See *Mingren zhuanji* 1978, 640. More distantly, Benjun was related to Tu Long 屠隆 (1543–1605), today of much greater literary fame. Born less than a year apart, Benjun and Long were respectively tenth- and ninth-generation descendants of the Southern Song scholar Tu Ji 屠季 (dates unknown) who had first put down roots in the region. For correspondence between the pair, see Tu Long 2012, vol. I, 309–310; vol. II, 166–167; 245; vol. IV, 324–325, 345–346.

67 Specifically in relation to *The Mountain-Forest Administrator's Companion* from 1608 (see below), which includes *Outer Sayings* (Tu Benjun 1988, 173).

68 Tu Benjun 1939.

69 Tu Benjun 1988, 315–330. It was also disseminated in compilations by others, for example in Mao Jin 1988, 473–492.

The Mountain-Forest Administrator's Companion was a project from Tu's retirement years, and was the first and only extant premodern work to collect all three *Master Mugwort* compilations in one place. The work, whose introduction is signed 1608, was printed by the Studio of Dedication to Virtue (Dunde tang 惇德堂) with heavy involvement from a contemporary named Chai Maoxian 柴懋賢, who possibly acted as the representative on the printshop or publishing house side. Certainly, the work was intended to enter the marketplace, as opposed to just being for personal consumption, judging by its four lavish prefaces, which at the time tended to be commissioned primarily as market endorsements.[70] The book's concept is an intriguing one: it proposes to provide the reader with everything they would need to know to embark on an eremitic life away from the constraints of society—or at least the official career track—by equipping them with an eclectic set of information: biographies of hermits from the past as models; practical advice on seasonal vegetables and the like; food for thought in the form of reading material (this is where the *Mugwort*s came in); and entertainment, in which instructions for literary drinking games feature heavily.

The Mountain-Forest Administrator's Companion also houses the three *Master Mugwort* collections translated in this volume, which are the first three constituents of a group of five texts under the overall title *Jest Intrigues of the Five Masters*, followed by Geng Dingxiang's 耿定向 (1524–1596) *Master Quan* (*Quanzi* 權子), and *Master Simple* (*Hanzi* 憨子) of Tu Benjun's own composition. The preface to *Jest Intrigues* places Master Mugwort's "sharp wits" on a par with the Humorists in *Records of the Historian* and compares his "polished diction" to that of the persuaders in the *Intrigues of the Warring States*. Indeed, the *Intrigues* connection has been placed paramount in his chosen title. More on Tu's thinking on the intended purpose of the *Jest Intrigues* is revealed in "On the Genesis of This Book" (*xuji yuanqi* 敘籍原起): "These 'Intrigues,' with their jocularity and effusions of jibes, are something that free-thinkers and eremitic gentlemen will be fully able to appreciate and laugh along with. But it is a book of fantastical unboundedness: when those stuck-in-my-ways geezers and veteran scholar-prudes see it, they will lose their heads in rage!"[71] More directly, Tu's preface to the *Jest Intrigues* collection discusses the place of remonstrative humor and satire within the Chinese tradition up until his time. While not strictly a preface to the *Mugwort* collections alone, this composition

---

70 By Li Weizhen 李維楨 (1547–1626), Shen Taichong 沈泰沖 (later Shen Fengchao 鳳超), Wang Sishi 王嗣奭 (1566–1648) and Chai Maoxian.

71 Tu Benjun 1988, 173.

is a key to how we should understand the *Mugwort* literary tradition as a whole and is translated in full in Appendix 2.[72]

Several of Tu's other works were compiled into Tao Ting's (*jinshi* 1610) *Environs of Fiction, Continued* (*Shuofu xu* 說郛續), a compendium that also included *Further Sayings*.[73] These include an appraisal of writings on seafood, guides to wild vegetables and seasonal flowers, and instructions for a drinking game. Beyond that, in his repertoire it is possible to detect a particular interest in the *Verses of Chu* (*Chuci* 楚辭), on which he produced several works including a revised edition of Song literatus Wu Renjie's 吳仁傑 explanatory notes on the vegetation that appears in the text, with supplementary notes.[74]

A penchant for humor is a distinctive trait across Tu's surviving works, even in places one might not expect to find it, such as the prefaces to his reference compilations.[75] Later in life he took the lighthearted sobriquet of "Old Simpleton" (Hansou 憨叟). Tu had an obvious fondness for playing with his chosen self-identifier of "simple" (*han* 憨), as seen in the title *Master Simple*; his introduction to *Book-satchel of Tea-leaves* opens, "This talentless fellow was born a simpleton, with little in the way of indulgent hobbies. Only with regard to the tea leaf is he unable to restrain himself."[76] Another surviving humorous work called *Insights from Deafness* (*Long guan* 聾觀) is comprised of a charismatic set of essays from around 1618 that describes the wonderful peace and quiet of life after losing his hearing in old age.[77] In *Outer Sayings*, therefore, we are looking at the brushstrokes of a seasoned humorist.

Note on the texts

This translation of *Miscellaneous Stories of Master Mugwort* is based on the edition titled *The Resident of East Slope's "Miscellaneous Stories of Master Mugwort"* (*Dongpo jushi "Aizi zashuo"* 東坡居士艾子雜說) in the *Fiction from Mr. Gu's Studio* (*Gushi wenfang xiaoshuo* 顧氏文房小說) edition,

---

72   For a discussion of the preface, see Smithrosser 2021, 147–160.
73   Tao Ting 1995–1997, 324–329.
74   Wu Renjie 1995.
75   For example, the aforementioned dictionary of Southeastern seafood opens, "Now, among aquatic lifeforms, none are as numerous as the fishes. In the realm of nomenclature, nothing has as much variety as the fishes. With regard to size, no animal is as large as the fishes. And when it comes to flavors, none are more delicious than the fishes(!)" (Tu Benjun 1939, 2).
76   Tu Benjun 1988, 315.
77   Wu Xiangxiang 1966, 2479–2506.

compiled by Gu Yuanqing 顧元慶 (1487–1565).[78] Punctuation generally follows the 1967 printing of a modern publication of the Gu edition in *Nine Works from "New Stories for Trimming Wicks" and Others* (*"Jiandeng xinhua" deng jiuzhong* 剪燈新話等九種).[79] Another important, abridged, edition is found in the *Environs of Fiction* (*Shuofu* 說郛).[80] Differences between editions are minimal, and other editions are helpful in resolving undocumented character variants and misprints. There is also an abridged version in *The Mountain-Forest Administrator's Companion*, in which Tu Benjun includes twenty-five episodes; given the proliferation of other editions, it is more likely that this is Tu's own selection rather than a reprint of a pre-existing abridged edition.[81] The "Stories" (*shuo* 說) part of the title found in the earlier editions begins to vary in the Ming.[82] *The Mountain-Forest Administrator's Companion* title swaps "Stories" for "Sayings" (*yu* 語), presumably to create cohesion among the three. Thus another extant edition, prefaced 1608, exists under the title *Miscellaneous Sayings of Master Mugwort* (*Aizi zayu* 艾子雜語).[83]

The translation of *Further Sayings* is based on the 1590 imprint of *Tales from the Fogged-Up World* (*Yanxia xiaoshuo* 煙霞小說), prefaced by Fan Qin 范欽 (1506–1585).[84] Notably, this edition did not include titles for the individual episodes.[85] A modern reprint can be found in *Nine Works from "New Stories for Trimming Wicks" and Others*; notwithstanding a few minor edits, my translation follows the punctuation supplied by this edition.[86] Premodern editions include Tao Ting's *Environs of Fiction, Continued* and

---

78 See Gu Yuanqing 1960, vol. II, 300–308. This is the longest version accessible to me. It is known that Zhao Kaimei's 趙開美 (1563–1624; later Zhao Qimei 琦美) edition carries a fortieth episode, with the title "A Qin scholar is fond of antiquity" (秦士好古), while during the Yuan dynasty, forty-one episodes were mentioned. See Li Ye 1935, 140 and Zhou Jin 2017, 5–6.

79 Yang Jialuo 1967, ch. 4. Pagination internal to chapter.

80 Su Shi 1986, 806–810.

81 See Tu Benjun 1988, 352–358. Given the context of this volume and his discussion of *Master Mugwort* in the preface, it is possible that Tu expected readers to be familiar enough with the content of *Miscellaneous Stories* and thus deemed it unnecessary to have printing blocks carved for the full text.

82 One example of this is *Miscellaneous Records of Master Mugwort* (*Aizi zaji* 艾子雜記), in Zhao Kaimei's 1602 imprint as part of *Five Assorted Works by East Slope* (*Dongpo zazhu wuzhong* 東坡雜著五種). See Liu Shangrong 1988, 132–164.

83 Tu Benjun 1988, 352.

84 Fan Qin 1995, 644–648. One of Tu Benjun's five sisters was married to Fan Qin's son, who at very least possessed a copy of *Tales from the Fogged-Up World*. The union is recorded in a grave inscription for Tu Dashan (see Shen Yiguan 1995–1997, 329). While mere speculation, it is certainly not impossible that Tu first came across *Further Sayings* in the library of his father- or brother-in-law.

85 See Appendix 3 for the titles in other versions of *Further Sayings*.

86 Yang Jialuo 1967, ch. 5.

an abridged version in *The Mountain-Forest Administrator's Companion*.[87] A later Chongzhen (1627–1644) edition is also known, as part of the *Collected Teases of Eight Gentlemen* (*Bagong youxi congtan* 八公遊戲叢談).[88]

The base reference edition for the translation of *Outer Sayings* is *The Mountain-Forest Administrator's Companion*.[89] This appears to be the only extant edition. A modern reprint can be found in *Nine Works from "New Stories for Trimming Wicks" and Others*; notwithstanding a few minor edits, my translation follows the punctuation supplied by this edition.[90]

The Translation

Context

In light of the often cryptic quality of these humorous collections, some-times indented notes are provided before and/or after the episode. Foot-notes provide basic glosses, with text-critical endnotes reserved for textual and translation issues or extra information such as alternative translations of the poems. However, the aim of this volume is to supply a translation of these texts, not an analysis; therefore its supplementary material has not attempted to be exhaustive, nor to present the only possible or definitive way of interpreting the satire or punchline. The reader is, as ever, welcome to form their own interpretation of the text. In fact, that is precisely my hope as translator: that this volume will encourage further engagement with what has hitherto been an understudied textual tradition of premod-ern Chinese literature.

Existing Translations

There is a smattering of English-language translations of individual *Master Mugwort* episodes across various anthologies, from *Miscellaneous Stories* in particular, and with a strong tendency towards those episodes in which the humor translates readily into English. Notably, William Dolby's *Chi-nese Humour: An Anthology*, a two-volume anthology of translations of humor across different genres, contains a total of ten episodes from *Mis-cellaneous Stories*.[91] Six episodes from *Miscellaneous Stories* and two from *Further Sayings* were translated by Jon Kowallis in *Wit and Humor from Old*

---

87 Tu Benjun 1988, 359–362.
88 Yang Jialuo 1967, ch. 5, 2.
89 Tu Benjun 1988, 363–370.
90 See Yang Jialuo 1967, ch. 6. In the case of *Outer Sayings*, readers should be wary of char-acter typos when consulting this reprint.
91 Dolby 2005, vol. I, 152–160. Specifically, MS:2, 5, 10, 13, 16, 17, 28, 30, 31, 39.

Cathay.[92] Lu Yunzhong 盧允中 also included two episodes from *Further Sayings* in *100 Chinese Jokes Through the Ages*.[93] Beyond that, occasional English translations of individual episodes are scattered far and wide. I have yet to encounter any pre-existing English translations of episodes from *Outer Sayings*.[94] In Japanese, Matsueda Shigeo 松枝茂夫 (1905–1995) translated a total of nineteen *Miscellaneous Stories* episodes, ten *Further Sayings* episodes, and ten *Outer Sayings* episodes as part of his 1970 collection *Selection of Jokes Through the Ages* (*Rekidai shōwasen* 歷代笑話選).[95]

92 Kowallis 1986, 24–29. Specifically, MS:16, 23, 26, 29, 31, 32; FS:6, 11.
93 Lu Yunzhong 1985, 13–17. Specifically, FS:6 and FS:9.
94 Smithrosser 2021 contains my previous translations of MS:5, 6, 12; FS:1, 6, 11, 13; and OS:18, as well as a few other shorter quotes. These are superseded by the versions in this volume.
95 Specifically, from *Miscellaneous Stories*, MS:1, 2, 4–8, 12, 15, 22, 23, 25, 26, 28, 29, 31–34. From *Further Sayings*, FS:2–4, 6, 8, 9, 11–14. From *Outer Sayings*, OS:1–3, 6–8, 11, 16, 17, 20.

.

The Misadventures of Master Mugwort

艾子雜說

[MS:1]

艾子事齊王。一日，朝而有憂色。宣王怪而問之。對曰：「臣不幸，稚子屬疾，欲謁告。念王無與圖事者，所朝，然心實係焉。」王曰：「盍早言乎？寡人有良藥，稚子頓服其愈矣。」遂索以賜。艾子拜受而歸。飲其子。辰服，而巳卒。他日，艾子憂甚戚。王問之故，慨然曰：「卿喪子可傷！賜卿黃金以助葬。」艾子曰：「殤子不足以受君賜。然臣將有所求。」王曰：「何求？」曰：「只求前日小兒得效方。」

---

1   More literally, the son was given the medicine during the *chen* 辰 period of the day (approx. 7–9am) and died soon after in the *si* 巳 period (approx. 9–11am).

Miscellaneous Stories of Master Mugwort

Master Mugwort is bestowed some excellent medicine (MS:1)

The first episode of the collection, like the first of each of the Ming sequels, finds our protagonist at the court of the King of Qi. The State of Qi is treated as Mugwort's primary base, with his (mis)adventures elsewhere generally taking place on his travels or in the context of an envoy mission.

Master Mugwort was in the service of the King of Qi. At court one day, the King noticed he had an anxious look about him. Finding this very much out of character, he inquired as to why.

"I'm afraid to say your servant is suffering a misfortune—my infant son is dangerously unwell," replied Master Mugwort. "I had intended to make my excuses today, but not wishing to leave my King without a minister with whom to plan affairs, I have presented myself at court. Truth be told, my thoughts are wrapped up in the other matter."

"Why didn't you say so earlier?" exclaimed the King, "We happen to have taken some medicine lately, and it worked like a charm! Go give your little boy a dose and he'll be cured."

The King had the medicine sought out posthaste and bestowed it upon Master Mugwort, who bowed low to accept his lord's gift before heading back home. He had his son drink the medicine, and the boy was dead within the hour.[1]

A few days thereafter, Master Mugwort presented himself at court in a very forlorn state indeed. After hearing the reason, the King said mournfully, "My dear minister. You must be so terribly sorry to have lost your son. We shall present you with some gold to cover the funeral costs."

"The death of a son is hardly reason enough to warrant such a gift from one's lord," said Master Mugwort. "Though your servant does have one small wish."

"What might that be?"

"Only that that 'excellent medicine' of yours had been the right prescription!"[2]

---

2 The Northern Song was a time of great upheaval in state policy; this episode seems to be a criticism of blanket implementations of policy across the land that did not take regional circumstances into consideration, as well as of "medicines" issued from above without a thorough investigation of the social issue they were intended to cure.

[MS:2]

艾子行於海上，見一物圓而褊，且多足。問居人曰：「此何物也？」曰：「蝤蛑也。」卽又見一物，圓褊多足。問居人曰：「此何物也？」曰：「螃蟹也。」又於後得一物，狀貌皆若前所見，而極小。問居人曰：「此何物也？」曰：「彭越也。」艾子喟然歎曰：「何一蟹不如一蟹也！」

[MS:3]

艾子使於魏；見安釐王。王問曰：「齊，大國也，比年息兵，何以為樂？」艾子曰：「敝邑之君好樂，而羣臣亦多效伎。」安釐王曰：「何人有伎？」曰：「淳于髡之籠養，孫臏之踢毬，東郭先生之吹竽，皆足以奉王歡也。」安釐王曰：「好樂不無橫賜，奈侵國用何？」艾子曰：「近日却告得孟嘗君處，借得馮驩來，索得幾文冷債，是以饒足也。」

3　More literally, "A crab never lives up to the previous crab." This is a play on "A given generation never lives up to the previous one" (*yidai buru yidai*, 一代不如一代), a remark on the general perception of an inability of younger members of society to live up to the older ones, and by extension, perhaps, the propensity of members an older generation to point out the deficiencies of the subsequent ones.

4　King Anxi of Wei ruled during some of the bloodiest years of the Warring States period, which saw his state pitted against its western neighbor Qin several times.

Master Mugwort asks about crabs (MS:2)

Master Mugwort was walking along the coast when his eyes fell upon a crustacean of some kind. It was round and flat and had many legs. "What is this thing?" he asked a passing local.

"That would be a sirloin crab."

Then he spotted another crustacean that was also round and flat with many legs. "What about this one?" he inquired.

"That's a cutlet crab."

After that, he caught sight of yet another one, which shared the same features as the others but was exceedingly tiny. "What about that?" he asked.

"A mincemeat crab."[i]

Master Mugwort sighed deeply and said, "Disappointing, isn't it, how things only seem to get worse as we go along!"[3]

King Anxi asks Master Mugwort about Qi (MS:3)

Master Mugwort was sent as a state envoy to Wei. At an audience with King Anxi, the King had a question for him: "Your state, Qi, is one of the largest in the world. Seeing as there has been a ceasefire of late, how do you pass the time?"[4]

"The lord of my land is partial to entertainment," replied Master Mugwort. "Among the ministerial throng, there are several who put on talent performances for him."

"Which ones?"

"There is Chunyu Kun with his caged birds, Sun Bin and his foot-juggling, and Master Dongguo who plays the pipes. Their talents are amusement enough for the King."

"When a ruler is partial to entertainment, he is invariably in the habit of handing out gifts willy-nilly," remarked King Anxi. "Do funds remain in the event of invasion by another state?"

"Well," replied Master Mugwort, "Recently we reported the matter to the Lord of Mengchang, who lent us the services of his retainer Feng Huan. He went about chasing up a few old debts—that should be more than enough!"

Rather than using the hard-earned peacetime to prepare for the inevitability of future wars, here an unnamed King of Qi is shown to squander state funds and indulge in watching the flagrantly lackluster performances of his courtiers, each of whom is singularly inept at his role. When Chunyu Kun was entrusted with a swan-goose to present to the King of Chu, he let it go en route instead.[5] Sun Bin

5   Nienhauser 1994–, vol. XI, 176–177; *Records of the Historian* 126.3197.

[MS:4]

齊地多寒。春深，求笋甲。方立春，有村老挈苜蓿一筐，以
與艾子。且曰：「此物初生，未敢嘗，乃先以薦。」艾子喜
曰：「煩汝致新。然我享之後，次及何人？」

　　曰：「獻公罷，卽刈以餵驢也。」

[MS:5]

艾子好飲，少醒日。門生相與謀曰：「此不可以諫止。唯以
險事怵之，宜可誡。」一日，大飲而噦。門人密抽彘腸致噦
中，持以示曰：「凡人具五臟方能活。今公因飲而出一臟，
止四臟矣。何以生耶？」艾子熟視而笑曰：「唐三藏猶可活，
況有四耶！」

---

6   Yang and Li 1982, 326–327.

7   See Nienhauser 1994–, vol. VII, 358–360; *Records of the Historian* 75.2359–2363. This figure appears as Feng Huan in *Records of the Historian* and as Feng Xuan 馮諼 in the *Intrigues*.

was a military strategist in the service of Qi, who was famously kneecapped as a punishment for a crime he did not commit during his early career, which permanently impaired his leg movement. The pipe-player Dongguo refers to the hermit Nanguo, a musician in the service of King Xuan, who is famous precisely for his lack of talent.[6] Finally, Feng Huan was once sent by the Lord of Mengchang as a debt collector, but he took payments only from those with the means to pay and burnt the debt tallies of those who did not.[7]

Master Mugwort receives a rare delicacy (MS:4)

The territory of Qi is prone to cold spells; even in the depths of spring nothing substantial has sprouted.[ii] Soon after the end of winter, an old man from the village called upon Master Mugwort with a basket of alfalfa and presented it to him.[8]

"This is the very first produce of the year. I wouldn't dare eat something like this myself, so I thought I'd come and offer it to you."

Master Mugwort was thrilled. "You went to the trouble of giving me the freshest batch!" he exclaimed, "Say—after I've enjoyed this special gift, who'll get the second batch?"

"Having presented the first batch to you, my good sir," replied the old man, "I'll be chopping up the rest for the donkey."

Master Mugwort's disciples stage an intervention (MS:5)

Master Mugwort was an avid drinker; rare were his sober days. His concerned disciples discussed the issue amongst themselves and settled on a plan: "We won't be able to get him to stop by confronting him directly about it. Instead, let's show him the peril of his ways by giving him a good scare. That'll do the trick."[iii]

One day, Master Mugwort drank too much and threw up. One of his disciples took his cue to discreetly pull out some pig guts and plant them in the puddle of vomit. Holding them up in front of his teacher's eyes, he gasped dramatically: "Regular mortals can only stay alive with all five of their vital organs in place.[9] But now it would appear that you have ejected one of them in your drunken state, and that leaves you with just four vital organs! How are you going to survive?!"

Master Mugwort inspected the intestines closely, laughed and said, "Sanzang of the Tang survived just fine. So I'm sure I'll be all right with four!"

Sanzang 三藏 refers to the Tang monk Xuanzang 玄奘 (602–664), best known to many readers from *Journey to the West* (*Xiyou ji* 西遊記), while *sanzang* 三臟 is a close match in both sound and form, and means "three organs," hence the pun.

---

8   "Alfalfa" or "lucerne" (*muxu*) is used around the world as animal feed.
9   The five viscera (*wuzang* 五臟), i.e., the heart, liver, spleen, lungs, and kidneys.

[MS:6]

艾子行出邯鄲道上，見二嫗相與讓路。一曰：「嫗幾歲？」
曰：「七十。」問者曰：「我今六十九。然則，明年當與爾同
歲矣。」

[MS:7]

艾子一夕疾，呼一人鑽火。久不至。艾子呼促之。門人曰：
「夜暗，索鑽具不得。」謂先生曰：「可持燭來，共索之矣。」
艾子曰：「非我之門，無是客也。」

[MS:8]

艾子見有人徒行，自呂梁託舟人以趨彭門者。持五十錢遺舟
師。師曰：「凡無賫而獨載者，人百金。汝尚少半。汝當自
此為我挽牽至彭門，可折半直也。」

---

10 Lüliang is a mountainous area 35km southeast of Pengmen, which is in present-day
      Xuzhou, Jiangsu province.
11 King Zhao is nowadays usually known as King Zhaoxiang 昭襄 of Qin. See MS:11.

Master Mugwort encounters two old women (MS:6)

Master Mugwort was out traveling down the road to Handan. There he saw two old women deciding who should give way to whom based on seniority.

Said the first, "Old dear, how old are you?"

Said the second, "Seventy."

Said the first, "I'm sixty-nine. But give it a year and I'll have caught up with you!"

Master Mugwort hollers for his disciple (MS:7)

Master Mugwort was unwell one night. He hollered for someone to light a fire, but after quite some time no assistance had arrived. Master Mugwort called out again to hurry things along.

"It's dark tonight," responded the disciple, "and I've been looking all over for the fire-starting tools, but I just can't find them. Perhaps I should say, Venerable Sir, 'How about you bring a candle over so we can look together?'"

Master Mugwort said, "This one could only be a disciple of my own!"

This episode possibly plays on a preexisting anecdote that begins similarly, with the man falling ill in the night and calling on his servant to light a fire, but the tools cannot be found in the dark. Just like Mugwort does here, the master nags his servant, and when the servant asks him to help look, the master snaps back, "Well, if I had a light, what business would I have asking you look for them?!"[iv] The *Mugwort* version is resolved more harmoniously: when the disciple points out the parallel through his remark, Mugwort's response turns the irascible answer of the original to a congenial one which acknowledges his own error.

A boat to Pengmen (MS:8)

Master Mugwort saw a traveler journeying on foot. At Mount Lüliang, he decided to entrust a leg of his trip to a ferryman, so as to get to Pengmen a little sooner.[10] He turned over fifty coins to the ferryman, who retorted, "The fare for one person without luggage is one hundred, so you're short by half. But I can give you a half-price discount, buddy—all you have to do in return is tow the boat from here to Pengmen yourself!"

The Marquis of Rang loses a deer (MS:9)

Before King Zhao of Qin came of age, Wei Ran was the most powerful man in the state, steering the bulk of state policy as the king's maternal uncle and de facto regent.[11] He grew immensely rich and was instrumental in the military campaigns that paved the way for the First Emperor's success in unifying the states some decades later. But this was not to last.

[MS:9]

穰侯與綱壽接境，魏冉將以廣其封也，乃伐綱、壽而取之。兵回，而范睢代其相矣。艾子聞而笑曰：「眞所謂『外頭赶兔，屋裏失獐』也。」

[MS:10]

齊王一日臨朝，顧謂侍臣曰：「吾國介於數强國間，歲苦支備，令（今）欲調丁壯築大城，自東海起。連即目，經太行，接轘轅，下武關，透迤四千里，與諸國隔絕，使秦不得窺吾西，楚不得竊吾南，韓、魏不得持吾之左右，豈不大利邪？

---

12 Areas in modern-day Shandong province.

13 Also commonly written as Fan Ju 范雎. See also *Fan Sui is granted an audience with King Zhao* (MS:19). For a compilation of *Intrigues* and *Records of the Historian* translations relating to Fan Sui, see Crump 1998, 16–36.

The fiefdom of Wei Ran, the Marquis of Rang, bordered on Gang and Shou.[12] Thinking to expand his lands, the Marquis invaded Gang and Shou and annexed them. But when he returned with his troops, he found that Fan Sui had replaced him as Prime Minister.[13]

When news of this reached Master Mugwort, he laughed and said, "Truly 'Heading out to catch a rabbit, and losing a deer from back home' as they say!"

While Wei Ran was out of Qin deploying state troops for this self-serving purpose, a dark horse figure named Fan Sui seized his chance to send the king the letter that set in motion a series of events ending with him persuading King Zhao that the time had come to take back control over state decisions and assert his own dominance as ruler. Fan Sui was installed as prime minister while Wei Ran was booted out of the country.

The King of Qi designs a Great Wall (MS:10)

The unpredictable multistate environment forced states to maintain a constant state of preparedness for sudden attacks, which put considerable pressure on state resources and the morale of the people. Qi's eastern location with its stretch of coastline (see Map 1) was arguably more fortunate than that of the more central states like Wei and Hann, which were surrounded on all sides.

One day, the King of Qi was presiding over court business. Looking with glee at the ministers assembled before him, he announced, "Our State of Qi is bordered by several powerful states. Year after year we take great pains to ready ourselves for potential incursions. But things do not have to be this way. Let us take action today and conscript the young and able-bodied to build a great wall! The wall will start off at the Eastern Seas, link up with Jimu and pass along the Taihangs before reaching Mount Huanyuan and ending at the Wu Pass.[14] A wall like that would create a division between us and the other states for no less than four thousand miles. That way, Qin won't catch a peek of Our west, Chu will have no way to make a grab at Our south, and the stretch in between will be safely out of the clutches of Hann and Wei. Could it be any more

---

14 Jimu a.k.a. Jimo 卽墨, in Warring States Qi, just north of present-day Qingdao. The Taihangs are a mountain range running along the border between today's Hubei and Shanxi,
meeting Hunan at the south; they were the site of an important interstate route. Mount
Huanyuan is in present-day Henan province, and was the site of an important pass. Wu
Pass probably refers to an important pass between Qin and Chu, which make the stated
geography of the proposed wall a little odd. This could be a deliberate exaggeration of
the locations and scope of the wall, given that this plan is supposed to be the unfeasible
scheme of an out-of-touch king.

今百姓築城，雖有少勞，而異日不復有征戍侵虜之患，可以永逸矣。聞吾下令，孰不欣躍而來耶？」艾子對曰：「今旦大雪，臣趨朝。見路側有民，裸露僵踣，望天而歌。臣怪之，問其故。答曰：『大雪應候，且喜明年人食賤麥。我即今年凍死矣。』正如今日築城百姓，不知享永逸者在何人也。」

[MS:11]

艾子使於秦，還語宣王：「秦昭王有吞噬之心。且其狀貌，又正虎形也。」宣王曰：「何質之？」曰：「眉上五角聳，目光爛然，鼻直口哆，豐頤壯臆。每臨朝，以兩手按膝。望之，宛然鎮宅獅子也。」

---

15 The king's scheme is completely out of touch with the realities of his people's lived experience. See also *The King of Qi gives Master Mugwort some excellent medicine* (MS:1) and *Master Mugwort visits the Prime Minister of Qin* (MS:36).

beneficial for Qi and its people? To be sure, if the commonfolk have to build such a big wall it would mean a little toil for them in the short term. But in return, in days to come they will no longer have to worry about being sent far away to a border garrison or suffering invading forces. They'll be free of such worries forevermore! When We send out the edict, won't they all jump for joy and come running to volunteer themselves?"

To this, Master Mugwort replied, "This morning, there was heavy snow-fall. As your servant here hurried to court, he caught sight of a commoner by the side of the road. The fellow was lying there exposed and dying, yet he was gazing up at the Heavens, singing. I thought this peculiar, and so inquired as to the reason. He told me, 'This heavy snow has come exactly at the right point in the year. I'm stoked—we'll be eating wheat on the cheap next year. Too bad I'll be freezing to death before this year is out.' For the commonfolk who start building a wall today, it'll be just like that: who knows if there'll be any of them left to enjoy your worry-free eternity!¹⁵

Master Mugwort reports on King Zhao of Qin (MS:11)

King Zhao of Qin's long reign oversaw several large expansions of Qin territory and military successes that laid the groundwork for his great-grandson's eventual unification of the states.

Master Mugwort was sent on an envoy mission to Qin.

Upon his return, he told King Xuan, "I swear, that King Zhao of Qin is of a mind to gobble up the entire world. The man had the look of a tiger!"

Said King Xuan, "A tiger? How so?"

Said Master Mugwort:

Eyebrows arched up his forehead,
A flickering glint to the eyes,
Nose straight and mouth a-snarl,
Ample jaw and thick-set chest.
And whenever he was holding audience at court, he always sat with
    both hands planted on his knees. From afar, one might very well
    mistake him for a guardian lion statue!¹⁶

---

16 Guardian lion statues, previously known as "foo dogs" in English, are still a common sight at the entrances to buildings in China today. Lion figurines were placed in Tang tombs, and by the Song, large statues of bronze or stone were stationed at the entrance to certain residential and educational establishments, as well as inside the palace compound.

[MS:12]

艾子為莒守。一日，聞秦將以白起為將伐莒。莒之民悉欲逃
避。艾子呼父老而慰安之曰：「汝且弗逃。白起易與耳。且
其性仁。前且伐趙，兵不血刃也。」

[MS:13]

艾子曰：

「田巴居於稷下，是三皇而非五帝。一日屈千人。其辨無能
窮之者。弟子禽滑釐出，逢嫠媼，揖而問曰：『子非田巴之
徒乎？宜得巴之辨也。媼有大疑，願質于子。』滑釐曰：『媼
姑言之。可能折其理。』媼曰：『馬鬣生向上而短，馬尾
生向下而長，其故何也？』滑釐笑曰：『此殆易曉事，馬鬣
上搶，勢逆而強，故天使之短；馬尾下垂，勢順而遜，故天以
之長。』媼曰：『然則人之髮上搶，逆也，何以長？鬚下垂，
順也，何以短？』滑釐茫然自失。乃曰：『吾學未足以臻此。

---

17 Once a small state of its own, Ju with its walled city later became a stronghold of Qi.
18 Literally, "his soldiers did not bloody their blades."
19 Getting to the bottom of the "this" and the "not-this" *shi* 是 and the *fei* 非 was the goal of some disputations. See Fraser 2020. Tian Ba apparently has the audacity to apply such methods even to the hallowed god-kings and sage-rulers that were the Three Sovereigns and Five Emperors.
20 See "Persuasions and disputations" in the Introduction.

Master Mugwort prepares for a siege (MS:12)

Bai Qi was a Qin general with a fearsome reputation. The Battle of Changping, for example, is infamous for his mass slaughter of captured and surrendered Zhao populations. *Records of the Historian* reports a total of 450,000 deaths, the majority systematically buried alive in gigantic pits.

Master Mugwort was magistrate of Ju.[17] One day, word arrived that the State of Qin was going to march on Ju, led by none other than Bai Qi. The people of Ju scrambled to flee. Master Mugwort shouted to the elderly population to reassure them, "You lot won't be fleeing, but rest assured![V] Bai Qi will be a piece of cake. Plus, I hear he's a benevolent man! That time when he marched on Zhao, his soldiers didn't spill a single drop of blood!"[18]

The Lame Old Lady's puzzler (MS:13)

Master Mugwort said:

> Tian Ba was resident at the Jixia Academy. He was the type who'd affirm the Three Sovereigns and refute the Five Emperors themselves if you'd let him![19] In a single day he could subdue a thousand men in debate. When it came to the art of disputation, no one could exhaust his wordy acrobatics.[20]
>
> His disciple Qin Guli was heading out one day when he encountered a Lame Old Lady.[VI] She clasped her hands together to greet him and said: 'Well, if it isn't one of Tian Ba's disciples! You're sure to have a decent grasp of his disputations. This old lady has a puzzler for ya.'
>
> Said Guli, 'Old dear, do speak it. I shall endeavor to solve the matter by breaking it down to its underlying principles.'
>
> The Old Lady said, 'The mane of a horse grows upwards and is short, while its tail grows downwards and is long. What's the reason for this?'
>
> Guli chuckled and said, 'Why, that's very simple! The mane of a horse sticks upward, which means it possesses a forcefulness that defies its circumstance. Thus, Heaven keeps it short. And the tail of a horse droops downwards, which means it possesses a compliancy that conforms to its circumstance. Thus, Heaven grants it length.'
>
> The Old Lady said, 'But then again, the hair on a man's head also sticks upward. If that's because of its defiance, then why is it long? And his beard droops downward. If that's because of its compliancy, then why is it short?'
>
> Said Guli, 'I must admit, my level of learning leaves me ill equipped to get to the bottom of this one. I shall go back inside

當歸咨師。嫗幸專畱此。以須我還。其有以奉酬。』即入見田巴曰：『適出，嫛嫗問以駿尾長短。弟子以逆順之理答之，如何？』曰：『甚善。』滑釐曰：『然則，嫗申之以鬢順為短，髮逆而長，則弟子無以對。願先生折之。嫗方坐門以俟，期以餘教詔之。』巴俛首久之，乃以行呼滑釐曰：『禽大禽大，幸自無事也，省可出入。』」

[MS:14]

艾子曰：

「堯治天下，久而耄勤。呼許由以禪焉。由入見之。所居土堦三尺，茅茨不翦，采椽不斵。雖逆旅之居，無以過其陋。命許由食，則飯土䀌刑，啜土器，食龘糲，羹藜藿，雖廝監之養無以過其約。

to consult my teacher. Old dear, please remain here and await my return. I will come back out with an answer to your conundrum.'

With that, he went back inside to see Tian Ba and told him, 'Just now when I was heading out, the Lame Old Lady asked me about horses' manes being short and their tails being long. Your student gave an answer along the lines of the principle of defiance and compliance. How was that?'

'Very good,' agreed Tian Ba.

'But then, she asked a follow-up question about beards being compliant yet short, and hair being defiant yet long, and your student had naught by which to respond. I do hope you can solve it, Master. The Old Lady is sitting by the gates as we speak, eagerly awaiting our explanation.'

Tian Ba lowered his head and thought upon the matter at length. Sighing over his wayward disciple, he said 'Oh Qin, if you had nothing to do in the first place, why not have fewer comings and goings!'[vii]

All Under Heaven (MS:14)

Yao was a prehistoric monarch who was held up by Confucius and many other thinkers as a sage ruler and model for contemporaneous monarchs to aspire to. One of his celebrated traits was frugality. As related in the *Huainanzi* 淮南子, "When Yao possessed All Under Heaven . . . he lived with untrimmed thatching for a roof and unsanded oak for rafters, his carriage unadorned and his woven mat unhemmed . . . and when he passed down the entire world to Shun, he did so as easily as stepping backwards out of his slippers."[viii] But Shun was not the first man onto whom Yao attempted to offload his slippers. Xu You, the other figure who appears in this episode, had previously rejected the same offer.

Master Mugwort said:

> Yao had governed All Under Heaven for a very long time, reaching such an advanced age that he could no longer carry out his duties. He summoned Xu You, intending to cede the throne to him. Xu You entered an audience with the ruler, and found his abode to be an earthen-stepped hovel of just three feet, with untrimmed thatching for a roof and unsanded oak for rafters.[ix] Not even a roadside hostel could be so primitive! Yao bade Xu You to dine, and out came an earthenware crock and clay bowls, along with a bit of coarse unhulled grain paired with boiled goosefoot-weed and bean-leaves. Not even a bond servant's provisions could be so meager!

食畢，顧而言曰：『吾都天下之富，享天下之貴，久而厭矣。今將舉以授汝。汝其享吾之奉也。』許由顧而笑曰：『似此富貴，我未甚愛也。』」

[MS:15]

秦破趙於長平，坑衆四十萬。遂以兵圍邯鄲。諸侯救兵，列壁而不敢前，邯鄲垂亡，平原君無以為策。家居愁坐，顧府吏而問曰：「相府有何未了公事？」吏未對。新垣衍在坐，應聲曰：「唯城外一火竊盜未獲爾。」

21 See *Master Mugwort prepares for a siege* (MS:12).

22 On Xinyuan Yan, see Nienhauser 1994–, vol. VII, 519–525; *Records of the Historian* 83.2459–2465. For the quote, see Nienhauser 1994–, vol. VII, 373; *Records of the Historian* 76.2369.

Once Xu You had finished eating, Yao looked him in the eye and confessed his intention: 'I possess all the riches under Heaven and partake in all the treasures under Heaven.[x] But I have long since had my fill, and hereby confer everything upon you. Please accept my humble offering.'

Holding his gaze, Xu You laughed and said, 'If these are the riches and treasures you're talking about, I can't say I care much for them!'"[xi]

The Lord of Pingyuan's conundrum (MS:15)

Following its mass slaughter of Zhao soldiers at the Battle of Changping, Qin sent its armies to besiege the Zhao capital of Handan.[21] This was an era-defining moment: a seizure of Handan would be tantamount to the demise of the Zhao state. Its survival depended on the intervention of the surrounding states, including Chu and Wei, and for them, the choice of whether or not to send in their armies came down to whether the preservation of Zhao was worth incurring the wrath of the powerful Qin. This was a time of much deliberation and delay on the part of the surrounding states, while the enfeoffed lords of the area desperately maneuvered to persuade their kings to save Handan and ready their own retinues for battle. This episode, set amid the crisis, gives us a glimpse into the residence of Zhao's prime minister, the Lord of Pingyuan, as he awaits a resolution inside the city while the siege situation grows ever more dire.

Qin dealt Zhao a heavy blow at Changping and buried four hundred thousand of their men. After that, it lay siege to Handan. The relief troops of the various lords were dotted around the vicinity, but they had not yet dared issue the order to send them in. Handan was on the brink.

The Lord of Pingyuan was at a loss and sat fretfully at his residence. He turned to his clerk and demanded, "Are there any jobs left on the prime ministerial agenda?"

Before the clerk could reply, Xinyuan Yan, who was in attendance, piped up to say, "Just that one roving bandit at the city walls we haven't managed to deal with yet."[xii]

The siege of Handan was eventually lifted thanks to the advance of the relief troops, and the State of Zhao lived to see another day. Xinyuan Yan was a Wei envoy who was indeed present in the city; the irony here lies in the Lord of Pingyuan bringing up the day-to-day duties of his desk job even as families had reportedly started "exchanging their children to eat."[22] Eventually, the Lord of Pingyuan would arm his wives, concubines, and retainers and launch into an all-or-nothing charge at the Qin armies, which turned out to be just what it took to inspire the other relief troops to pile in and save Handan.

[MS:16]

公孫龍見趙文王，將以夸事眩之。因為王陳「大鵬九萬里」、「釣連鰲」之說。文王曰：「南海之鰲，吾所未見也。獨以吾趙地所有之事報子。寡人之鎮陽，有二小兒，曰東里，曰左伯，共戲于渤海之上。須臾，有所謂鵬者，羣翔於水上。東里遽入海以捕之。一攫而得。渤海之深，才及東里之脛。顧何以貯也？於是挽左伯之巾以囊焉。左伯怒，相與鬮之，久不已。東里之母，乃拽東里回。左伯舉太行山擲之，誤中東里之母，一目眯焉。母以爪剔出，向西北彈之。故太行中斷，而所彈之石，今為恒山也。子亦見之乎？」公孫龍逡巡喪氣，揖而退。弟（艾）子曰：「嘻，先生持大說以夸鉉人，宜其困也。」

---

23 Fraser 2020, 6.1. See also Graham 1989.
24 King Wen was also known as King Huiwen 惠文王. The two persuasions are extravagant stories about enormous mythical birds and turtles, though neither are usually associated with Gongsun Long. The roc persuasion is found in *Zhuangzi* (Ziporyn 2020, 3) and the gargantuan turtle story in *Liezi* (Graham 1973, 97–98; Yang Bojun 1979, 154).

Gongsun Long meets his match (MS:16)

Gongsun Long was in the service of the State of Zhao, where the following episode finds its setting. Han writers placed him into the "School of Names," or "Logicians," a category of otherwise unconnected thinkers who shared a concern with issues of linguistics, concepts, and beating their opponents into submission with clever arguments. Gongsun is best known for his association with his "A White Horse Is Not a Horse" paradox, which took five different logical approaches to attempt to force his listener to concede exactly that.[23]

Gongsun Long had an audience with King Wen of Zhao and was gearing up to overwhelm him with exaggerated extrapolations and reel off such persuasions as "The gigantic roc rises ninety thousand miles" and "Six gargantuan turtles in one fell swoop."[24]

King Wen remarked, "Well, I can't say I've ever seen a South Sea giant turtle. But I can tell you about what goes on in my Zhao! Have you heard how Zhao's mountains came into being? Once, two lads, one called Dongli, and the other Big Zuo, had been playing in the Bohai Sea for some time when a bunch of those birds you call rocs flew over the water.[25] Dongli waded nearer to catch one, lunged, and managed to get hold of one. The full depth of the Bohai Sea only came up to his shins! 'What can I use to wrap up the bird?' he asked himself. And so he gathered Big Zuo's headscarf together at the corners and bagged the bird. Big Zuo was indignant and the pair took to fisticuffs. After they had been at it for some time, Dongli's mom showed up to drag him back home, at which point Big Zuo picked up one of the Taihang mountains and flung it at Dongli, but he got his mom by mistake, blinding her in one eye! She gouged the mountain out with her fingernails and tossed towards the northwest. That's why there's a break in the Taihang range, and as for the rock she threw, it now stands as Mount Heng.[26] Have you ever heard such a thing?"

Gongsun Long was dumbstruck. Crestfallen, he made the requisite bow and then his exit.

Master Mugwort said to him, "Hah! Venerable Sir, overwhelming the opponent with grand persuasions is your signature move! No wonder you're gobsmacked."[xiii]

---

25 Big Zuo is the eldest son of the Zuo family. The Bohai Sea is the gulf north of Shandong.
26 In Warring States Zhao and present-day Shanxi.

[MS:17]

營丘士，性不通慧。每多事，好折難而不中理。一日，造
艾子問曰：「凡大車之下，與橐駝之項，多綴鈴鐸，其故何
也？」艾子曰：「車駝之為物，其大，且多夜行，忽狹路相
逢，則難於回避。以藉鳴聲相聞，使預得回避爾。」營丘士
曰：「佛塔之上，亦設鈴鐸，豈謂塔亦夜行而使相避邪？」
艾子曰：「君不通事理乃至如此。凡鳥鵲多託高以巢，糞穢
狼藉。故塔之有鈴，所以警鳥鵲也。豈以車駝比邪？」營丘
士曰：「鷹鷂之尾，亦設小鈴。安有鳥鵲巢於鷹鷂之尾乎？」
艾子大笑曰：「怪哉，君之不通也！夫鷹準擊物，或入林中
而絆足，縚線偶為木之所綰，則振羽之際，鈴聲可尋而索
也。豈謂防鳥鵲之巢乎？」營丘士曰：「吾嘗見挽郎秉鐸而
歌。雖不究其理，今乃知恐為木枝所綰，而便於尋索也。抑
不知綰郎之足者，用皮乎？用線乎？」艾子慍而答曰：「挽
郎乃死者之導也。為死人生前好詰難，故鼓鐸以樂其尸耳。」

Master Mugwort is challenged to a logical duel (MS:17)

The next episode recounts an attempt at the kind of disputative acrobatics for which Gongsun Long is renowned made by a scholar in possession of neither his talent nor his showmanship.[xiv]

The Scholar of Yingqiu was dense by nature.[27] He was a constant busybody who loved nothing more than to pose disputations to the detriment of basic logic. One day, he paid Master Mugwort a visit to ask, "On the underside of carriages and on the nape of camels' necks, one finds, in many instances, bells attached. Why is this the case?"

"Carriages and camels are very large things and they often travel by night," began Master Mugwort. "If they suddenly came face-to-face on a narrow road, they would be hard pressed to avoid bumping into one another. But with the ringing of the bells they can hear each other before that happens, allowing them to get out of each other's way in advance."

The Scholar of Yingqiu had his counter-argument ready. "But then again, one also finds bells installed at the top of Buddhist pagodas," he retorted. "Surely this cannot mean the pagodas go traveling by night and the bells help them to get out of each other's way!"

"It would seem that the logic of matters is utterly lost on you!" replied Master Mugwort. "Birds build their nests in high places like pagodas, and when they do, their filthy droppings get all over the place. Thus, people install the bells to scare the birds away. How could you compare that to the case of carriages and camels?"

"But then again, one also finds little bells tied onto the tails of hawks," countered the Scholar of Yingqiu. "As if another bird could build its nest upon the tail of a hawk!"

Master Mugwort roared with laughter and said, "How bizarrely dense you are! When a hawk strikes its prey, sometimes it flies into the woods and the string attached to its foot can get tangled up in the trees. As the bird flaps about, the bell on its tail rings out and its master can trace the sound to find it. As if that bell could be to deter nesting birds!"

"But then again, I once saw a dirge-lad ringing bells and singing," replied the Scholar of Yingqiu. "I cannot quite see why, but I suppose he must have been worried about getting tangled up in tree branches somehow, and was just trying to make himself easy to trace. Anyway, were they bound to his feet with leather? Or with string?"

Now irritated, Master Mugwort replied, "That was for still another reason. The dirge-lad clears the way for the coffin during the funeral procession. In life, the deceased happened to be just as fond of asking questions as your good self. And the bells—they must have been there to keep his corpse entertained."

[MS:18]

趙以馬服君之威名，擢其子括為將，以拒秦。而適當武安君
白起。一戰軍破。掠趙括，坑其眾四十萬。邯鄲幾敗。艾子
聞之曰：「昔有人將獵而不識鶻，買一鳧而去。原上兔起，
擲之使擊。鳧不能飛，投于地。再擲，又投於地。至三四，
鳧忽蹣跚而人語曰：『我鴨也，殺而食之，乃其分。奈何加
我以抵擲之苦乎？』其人曰：『我謂爾為鶻，可以獵兔耳。
乃鴨耶？』鳧舉掌而示，笑以言曰：『看我這脚手，可以搦
得他兔否？』」

---

28 For more on Changping, see *Master Mugwort prepares for a siege* (MS:12), and *The Lord of Pingyuan's conundrum* (MS:15).
29 See *The Marquis of Rang loses a deer* (MS:9).

Hunting with ducks (MS:18)

The catastrophic defeat of Zhao at the hands of Qin at Changping has been attributed not just to the prowess of the Qin general Bai Qi, but equally to the ineptitude of the Zhao side, especially the Zhao king's ill-advised decision to replace a more experienced general with Zhao Kuo, for little reason other than his pedigree as son of the late tax-collector-turned-general Zhao She, the Lord of Mafu, who had once saved a portion of Zhao territory from Qin against great odds.[28]

The State of Zhao selected Zhao Kuo as their general to repel Qin forces on account of the mighty reputation of his father, the Lord of Mafu. But he happened to come up against Bai Qi, the Lord of Wu'an, who defeated his army in an instant, slaying Zhao Kuo and burying four hundred thousand of his men alive. Later, Handan was very nearly lost.

When Master Mugwort heard of this, he said:

> Once upon a time, there was a man who was getting ready to go hunting. The man knew little about falcons, so he bought a duck and went on his way. When a rabbit hopped up on the prairie, he flung the duck at it to prompt it to fly and strike the rabbit. But the duck could not fly and just flopped to the ground. He made another duck-flinging attempt, and once again it flopped right back to the ground.
>
> After the third and fourth try, the duck abruptly got up, waddled over and said in a human voice, 'I am a duck! Something to be killed and eaten—such is my lot in life. So what business do you have piling on extra suffering by hurling me about beforehand?'
>
> The man said, 'I thought you were a falcon for hunting rabbits, but you're actually a duck?'
>
> The duck raised his wings to show the man, then laughed and said, 'Look at these hands and feet of mine. As if they could snatch up a rabbit!'"

Mugwort's remark, which presents the duck in a much more sympathetic light than the hunter, places the blame for this era-defining loss squarely on the King's shoulders for choosing the wrong man for the job.[XV]

Fan Sui is granted an audience with King Zhao (MS:19)

As we have seen, King Zhao of Qin had been a child king whose early reign was overseen by regents, and even after he reached manhood, state control remained largely in their hands.[29] He was finally persuaded to exile most of the clique by a man by the name of Fan Sui, who told the young king cautionary tales of the gruesome fates that had befallen past kings who permitted certain courtiers to wield power above their station.

[MS:19]

范雎一見秦昭王，而怵之以近禍。昭王遂幽太后，逐穰侯，廢高陵華陽君。於是秦之公族與羣臣，側目而憚雎。然以其寵，而未敢害之。一旦，王稽及鄭安平叛，而雎當緣坐。秦王念未有以代之者，尚緩其罪。因下令：「敢有言鄭安平叛者死。」然雎固已畏攝而不敢寧矣。艾子因使人告之曰：「佛經有云：『若被惡人逐，墮落金剛山。念彼觀音力，如日虛空住。』空中非可久住之地，此一撲終在，但遲速之間耳。」雎聞，薦蔡澤自代。

30 Royal relatives and cronies of the Marquis.
31 Having advocated for both men in the past, by Qin law Fan was himself implicated in their crimes.

When Fan Sui was granted an audience with King Zhao of Qin, he frightened the king by suggesting he was heading for catastrophe. And so King Zhao placed the Queen Dowager under house arrest, expelled the Marquis of Rang, and discharged the Lords of Gaoling and Huayang.[30] As a result, the noble clans and ministers of Qin feared Sui and avoided looking him in the eye. But since he was the King's favorite, nobody dared maneuver against him.

When Wang Ji and Zheng Anping betrayed the King, Fan Sui was liable for punishment.[31] However, the King of Qin, mindful of the fact that he had no suitable replacement for Prime Minister, pardoned his crime by issuing an edict that proclaimed, "Anyone who dares mention the betrayal of Zheng Anping shall be executed." Still, the whole episode had long since instilled a sense of dread in Sui, and he did not dare take any solace in this.[xvi]

Given the situation, Master Mugwort sent a messenger to tell him, "There is a Buddhist sutra that says:

If you are chased by someone wicked
And he pushes you from Mount Diamond
Just focus your mind on the power of Avalokiteśvara
And you'll float in the air like the sun.[32]

But midair is not a place one can remain forever! The fall is a forgone conclusion—it is simply a matter of when!"

Upon hearing this, Fan Sui recommended Cai Ze as his replacement.[33]

Mugwort's quote of the *Lotus Sutra* comes from a chapter that exhorts those in all kinds of earthly trouble to focus their thoughts on or intone the name of the bodhisattva Avalokiteśvara (Guanyin), in the hope that (s)he will intervene and save the day. While this sutra promises devotees will be saved from a fall by magically floating in the sky, technically it omits mention of any safe delivery from that secondary predicament.

---

32 From "The Gateway to Every Direction (Manifested by Bodhisattva Avalokiteśvara)" (觀世音菩薩普門品) in the *Lotus Sutra* (*Miaofa lianhua jing* 妙法蓮華經). Mugwort has amalgamated two separate quotes into one. Translation adapted from Kubo and Yuyama 2007, 300.

33 Cai Ze did indeed replace Fan Sui as Prime Minister. In fact, it was Cai himself—and most certainly not Mugwort—who persuaded Fan to step down.

[MS:20]

艾子一日觀人誦佛經者，有曰：「呪咀諸毒藥，所欲害身者，念彼觀音力，還着於本人。」艾子喟然歎曰：「佛，仁也。豈有免一人之難，而害一人之命乎？是亦去彼及此。與夫不愛者何異也？」因謂其人曰：「今為汝體佛之意，而改正之可者乎？曰：『呪咀諸毒藥，所欲害身者，念彼觀音力，兩家都沒事。』」

[MS:21]

有人獻木履於齊宣王者，無刻斲之迹。王曰：「此履豈非生乎？」艾子曰：「鞿楦乃其核也。」

[MS:22]

齊宣王問艾子曰：「吾聞古有獬犭豹，何物也？」

艾子對曰：「堯之時，有神獸，曰獬豸，處廷中，辨

---

34   Translation adapted from Kubo and Yuyama 2007, 300.
35   Yao was a sage ruler in antiquity. See MS:14.

Master Mugwort overhears a Buddhist sutra (MS:20)

Another quote from that very section of the *Lotus Sutra* appears in the next episode:

One day, Master Mugwort was watching somebody recite a Buddhist sutra, which went:

> If someone is trying to maim you
> With a curse or with poison,
> Just focus your mind on the power of Avalokiteśvara,
> And these ills will rebound to afflict their authors![34]

Master Mugwort gave a heavy sigh and said, "Isn't the Buddha supposed to be a humane fellow? As if he would inflict harm upon the life of one person in order to spare another! If one avoids the misfortune only for it to befall another, how is that any different from being uncaring about the plight of one's fellow man?" And so he told the man, "How about I incorporate something of the Buddha's message for you by tweaking the words a little? It could go:

> If someone is trying to maim you
> With a curse or with poison,
> Then focus your mind on the power of Avalokiteśvara,
> And nothing will happen to either of you!"

King Xuan is presented with a pair of wooden shoes (MS:21)

Somebody presented King Xuan of Qi with a pair of wooden shoes that betrayed no signs of carving or chiseling.
    "What pristine shoes!" exclaimed the King. "It is as if they just grew that way!"
    "Then that would make the shoe last its pit," said Master Mugwort.

A shoe last was placed inside the shoe during the production process to form it into the correct size. If these shoes grew like fruit or nuts, then that would make the shoe last its stone or kernel.

King Xuan asks about the monoceros (MS:22)

"We have heard it said," King Xuan of Qi asked Master Mugwort, "that in ancient times there was a beast known as a 'monoceros'—pray, what was it like?"
    "In the time of Yao, there was a divine beast called a monoceros.[35] It was resident at court and could sniff out which among the ministerial

羣臣之邪僻者，觸而食之。」艾子對已，後進曰：「使今有此獸，料不乞食矣。」

[MS:23]

艾子浮于海，夜泊島嶼。中夜，聞水下有人哭聲，復若人言。遂聽之，其言曰：「昨日龍王有令：『應水族有尾者斬。』吾鼉也，故懼誅而哭。汝蝦蟆無尾，何哭？」復聞有言曰：「吾今幸無尾，但恐更理會科斗時事也。」

[MS:24]

艾子使於燕，燕王曰：「吾小國也，日為強秦所侵，徵求無已。吾國貧，無以供之。欲革兵一戰，又力弱不足以拒敵。如之何則可？先生其為謀之。」艾子曰：「亦有分也。」王曰：「其有說乎？」

艾子曰：「昔有龍王，逢一蛙於海濱。相問訊後，蛙問龍王曰：『王之居處何如？』王曰：『珠宮貝闕，暈飛璇題。』龍復問：『汝之居處何若？』

---

36 The monoceros (*xiezhi* 獬豸) was a mythological beast, described in one Han text as a "one-horned goat" that was put to use in proving the innocence or guilt of the suspect of a crime (Forke 1907, 321). Even today, it is a symbol of justice and law enforcement.

37 On the Dragon Kings, see Werner 1961, 292–297.

throng were wicked and corrupt. Then it would headbutt and devour them."

Then, with his reply technically complete, Master Mugwort couldn't resist adding one more thing: "And were that beast around in this day and age, I suspect it would not be in want of a good meal."[36]

Master Mugwort hears weeping in the sea (MS:23)

This is the first of a number of appearances in *Miscellaneous Stories* by one of the Dragon Kings. In general, Chinese literature depicts each king as having his own jurisdiction over the aquatic lifeforms of a particular region, complete with an underwater palace compound, typically at the bottom of the sea.[37]

Master Mugwort was sailing the seas. By night, he would moor his boat by the rocky islets. In the middle of the night, he heard the sound of weeping coming from the water. Then, he heard something that sounded like people talking. So he listened on and heard a voice say, "Yesterday the Dragon King issued an edict that declared, 'All water creatures with a tail shall be beheaded!' I'm an alligator, so I'm weeping because I'm afraid to die. But what's with you? You're a frog—you don't even have a tail! What are you crying for?" Master Mugwort heard another voice reply, "True, I am fortunate enough not to have a tail at present. But I'm terrified my past will come back to haunt me!"

The King of Yan's predicament (MS:24)

Master Mugwort was sent on an envoy mission to Yan. The King of Yan said, "Ours is a minor state. Day by day, the powerful Qin encroaches upon us with its relentless demands. But our state is poor, with nothing to offer in the way of tribute. Were We to send in the entirety of Our arms and troops to fight them, their collective power still wouldn't be enough to rebuff the enemy. This being the state of things, what should We do? Please do think upon the matter, Venerable Sir."

Master Mugwort said, "Being Yan has its own perks."

Said the King, "Do elaborate with a persuasion."

"Once upon a time," began Master Mugwort, "the Dragon King happened across a frog at the beach.

After the pair had introduced themselves and exchanged greetings, the Frog asked the Dragon King: 'So what is it like over at the King's residence?'

'Bepearled palaces and shell-adorned mansions, towering on high with jaded rafters,' answered the King. 'And what is it like at your residence?'

蛙曰：『綠苔碧草，清泉白石。』復問曰：『王之喜怒
如何？』龍曰：『吾喜則時降膏澤，使五穀豐稔。怒則先之
以暴風，次之以震霆，繼之以飛電，使千里之內，寸草不
雷。』龍問蛙曰：『汝之喜怒何如？』曰：『吾之喜則清風明
月，一部鼓吹；怒則先之以努眼，次之以腹脹，然後至於脹
過而休。』」於是，燕王有慚色。

[MS:25]

齊王於女，凡選婿，必擇美少年。顏長而白皙，雖中無所
有，而外狀稍優者，必取之。齊國之法，民為王婿，則禁與
士人往還。

38　With enviable highs come devastating lows: better to enjoy the tranquility afforded by
one's frog-like insignificance than hanker after a bigger stature. For another Yan-based
episode, see FS:2. For Yan in the *Intrigues*, see Crump 1996, 465–516; Liu Xiang 1978,
1039–1143.

'Green moss and emerald grasses, pristine springs and pure-white rocks,' answered the Frog. 'And what of Your joy and wrath, King?'

'When I am pleased, the rain falls with perfect seasonal timing, nourishing the soil so it produces a bumper harvest of every variety of staple grain. And as for my wrath, at first it brings about stormy gales, and then come the mighty thunderclaps, and after that lightning streaks through the sky, wreaking devastation across vast expanses survived not by a single blade of grass,' replied the Dragon. 'And what of your joy and wrath?'

'When I am pleased, there is a gentle breeze and a bright moon, and I ribbit a joyous tune. As for my wrath, at first my eyes bulge with rage, and then my belly inflates, and all that makes me feel a bit bloated so I just go and sleep it off.'

Upon hearing this, the King of Yan looked very ashamed of himself indeed.

If the State of Yan does not make a frequent appearance in the Master Mugwort collections, it is mostly due to the fact that its northerly position placed it out of the way of much of the major battles and political drama, and thus stories, of the Warring States. Here Mugwort gives the King of Yan a reality check. If Yan really were to gain the military might to which its king aspires, it would only invite trouble by drawing the eye of the other states.[38]

Qi's sons-in-law (MS:25)

The marriage of a ruler's daughters, of whom there were often many due to the numerous potential mothers, was no trivial matter in the functioning of a state. Premodern China regularly saw daughters given away in strategic marriage alliances with other states or, more often, the sons of powerful courtiers. The flipside to this was that such a union potentially meant access to the ruler, and with that came power and influence that could affect policy decisions, breed corruption, or even endanger the dynasty itself. Thus the question of sons-in-law sparked creative solutions like the one the State of Qi opts for in this episode.

When it came to selecting spouses for his daughters, the King of Qi would, without fail, go for the most beautiful among the choices. Even if a young man was irredeemably devoid of talent, so long as his visage was slender, fair, and bright, and his appearance finer than the rest, the King would be sure to pick him.

By the law of the land, in the event that a commoner became a royal son-in-law, he was from that day on prohibited from fraternizing with

唯奉朝請外，享美服珍味，與優伶為伍。但能奉其王女，則
為效矣。一日，諸婿退朝，相叙而行，傲然自得。艾子顧謂
人曰：「齊國之安危重輕，豈不盡在此數公乎？」

[MS:26]

齊有富人，家累千金。其二子甚愚。其父又不教之。一日，
艾子謂其父曰：「君之子雖美，而不通世務。他日曷能克其
家？」父怒曰：「吾之子敏而且恃多能，豈有不通世務耶？」
艾子曰：「不須試之他。但問君之子，所食者米，從何來。
若知之，吾當妄言之罪。」父遂呼其子問之。其子嘻然笑
曰：「吾豈不知此也。每以布囊取來。」其父愀然而改容曰：
「子之愚甚也！彼米不是田中來？」艾子曰：「非其父不生
其子。」

---

39 The son-in-law theme is revisited in *Master Mugwort meets the Dragon King of the Eastern Seas* (MS:28).

the men of service. When the sons-in-law of Qi weren't paying respects to the King at court, they spent their days dressing up in fancy outfits, enjoying the rarest of delicacies and partying with the court entertainers. [xvii] As long as a son-in-law attended well upon the King's daughter, he was considered to have served his purpose.

One day, a group of sons-in-law passed Master Mugwort on their way out of court, gossiping among themselves as they went, all haughty and self-satisfied. Master Mugwort looked towards the minister next to him and snorted, "Sure, why wouldn't we entrust all the matters of the Qi state— the peace and peril, the grave and the trivial—to this gaggle of princely laddies?"

The implied alternative here is to marry the daughters to men of service such as Master Mugwort himself, whose bitter remark at the end probably draws attention to how these men got to enjoy all the luxuries of court life without having to shoulder any state duties in return.[39]

Master Mugwort and the rich father (MS:26)

In Qi there was a wealthy individual whose household had piled up a thousand pieces of gold. But both of his sons were idiots, and moreover, the father showed no inclination to educate them.

One day, Master Mugwort said to the rich father, "Those boys of yours may be handsome, good sir, but they have no grasp of the way the world works. In the future, how are they going to do well by your fine household?"

"My sons are smart and have a great number of skills!" snapped the affronted father. "Their grasp of worldly matters leaves nothing to be desired."

"Then you need only test them by asking where the rice they eat comes from, my good sir," proposed Master Mugwort.[xviii] "And if they know, I'll be guilty of making a baseless claim."

So the father called one of his sons over and asked him the question.

The boy giggled and said, "How could we not know that! It gets scooped out of the big sack."

His father's face dropped. "Son, how could you be so dumb! Where else could it come from but the field?"

"Like father, like son," observed Master Mugwort.

The correct answer to the question of where the hulled and processed rice comes from would have involved the rice plant, or a description of the process from field to sack.

[MS:27]

鄒忌子說齊王。齊王說之，遂命為相。居數月，無善譽。艾
子見淳于髡問曰：「鄒子為相之久，無譽何也？」髡曰：「吾
聞齊國有一毛手鬼。凡為相，必以手摑之。其人遂忘平生忠
直，默默而已。豈其是歟？」艾子曰：「君之過矣！彼毛手
只擇有血性者摑之。」

[MS:28]

艾子一夕夢一丈夫，衣冠甚偉，謂艾子曰：「吾東海龍王
也，凡龍之產兒女，各與江海為婚姻，然龍性又暴，又以其
類同，少相下者。吾有小女，甚愛之。又其性尤戾。若吾女
更與龍為匹，

---

40 Not all stories show him in a negative light. See, for example, episode 119 of the *Intrigues*. Crump 1996, 164–165; Liu Xiang 1978, 324–327.

Master Mugwort asks Chunyu Kun about Zou Ji (MS:27)

Zou Ji was a powerful Qi minister during the reigns of King Wei and King Xuan. Accounts in the *Intrigues* and *Records of the Historian* portray him as a proud and manipulative figure prepared to use unscrupulous means to maintain his favorable position at court.[40] As the following episode hints, Zou Ji's ascent to power was sudden and unexpected: he was awarded the prime ministerial position by King Wei of Qi after accosting him with unsolicited advice on governance when invited to court to give a zither recital.

Master Zou Ji presented a persuasion to the King of Qi, who was delighted with it and thereupon conferred upon him the position of Prime Minister. Several months after the fact, his reputation was lacking.

When Master Mugwort had a meeting with Chunyu Kun, he asked, "Master Zou has been Prime Minister for quite some time now, yet he has no reputation to speak of. Why is that?"

"I have heard," began Chunyu Kun, "that the State of Qi is home to a Hairy-Handed Monster, and whenever we get a new Prime Minister, the Monster gives them a smack with those hands of his, and with that, the man utterly forgets all the loyalty and decency of his former life. All of a sudden, he goes quiet and no longer speaks out. Could it be that the Monster is behind it?"

"Good sir, you are mistaken!" exclaimed Master Mugwort. "Surely those hairy hands of his could only smack a fellow were he made of solid stuff to begin with!"[41]

Master Mugwort meets the Dragon King of the Eastern Seas (MS:28)

One night, Master Mugwort dreamed of a big fellow, dressed head-to-toe in a most stately manner. He had come to Master Mugwort for a consultation.

"I am the Dragon King of the Eastern Seas! Now, sons and daughters born of Dragons must each and every one be joined in matrimony with a creature from the rivers or seas. However, we Dragons are of a fiery temperament, so when we are paired with another of our kind, neither party will ever back down in a fight. My little girl, how I love her! Yet by nature she is very rebellious. If I wed her to another Dragon, we can say

---

41 More literally, "His hairy hands only pick full-blooded sorts (i.e., upstanding men with mettle) to smack." Mugwort's quip is thus a thinly veiled insult of Zou Ji, who in his view had no chance of being a good prime minister. No doubt such a remark would have been appreciated by Zou's rival Chunyu Kun. See Weingarten 2017, 510–512. Given Wang Anshi's relatively sudden ascent to power, it is possible that he is the target here.

必無安諧。欲求耐事而易制者，不可得。子多智，故來請問。姑為我謀之。」艾子曰：「王雖龍，亦水族也。求婿，亦須水族。」王曰：「然。」艾子曰：「若取魚，彼多貪餌，為釣者獲之，又無手足。若取黿鼉，其狀醜惡。唯蝦可也。」王曰：「無乃太卑乎？」艾子曰：「鰕有三德：一無肚腸，二割之無血，三頭上帶得不潔。是所以為王婿也。」王曰：「善。」

[MS:29]

艾子行水塗，見一廟矮小，而裝飾甚嚴。前有一小溝，有人行至水，不可涉。顧廟中，而輒取大王像，橫於溝上，履之而去。復有一人至，見之，再三嘆之曰：「神像直有如此褻慢！」乃自扶起，以衣拂飾，捧至坐上，再拜而去。須臾，艾子聞廟中小鬼曰：「大王居此以為神，享里人祭祀，反為愚民之辱。何不施禍以譴之？」

---

42 Fishbait is a metaphor for greedily chasing petty profits.
43 This could be one of the Four Great Heavenly Kings (*si da tianwang* 四大天王) from Buddhist mythology, generally depicted as fearsome figures and stationed at the threshold of temples and tombs as guardians.

goodbye to peace and harmony! I've been seeking a patient partner who will yield placidly to her control, but no luck yet. You are a wise fellow, so I came to seek advice. Do think on the matter for me!"

Master Mugwort said, "While you, King, are a Dragon, you remain a creature of the watery depths. Thus the son-in-law you seek must likewise be a creature of the waters."

Said the King, "That is so."

"Were you to choose a Fish, he would always be hankering after fishbait, and hence bound to be snatched from her by a fisherman.[42] Plus, that bunch have neither hands nor legs. And were you to choose a Turtle or Alligator, well, he would be too ugly. Only a Shrimp would fit the bill."

Said the King, "Would a Shrimp not be too lowly of a match?"

Said Master Mugwort, "There are three advantages to choosing a Shrimp. One, they have no guts. Two, if you cut them they don't bleed. Three, the top of their head is unclean. And that's why they'd make a good royal son-in-law."

"Excellent!" agreed the King.

The lack of "guts" is not a metaphor for having no courage, but rather for having little autonomy of thought and opinion. "Blood" is a metaphor for spiritedness or mettle. As for the unclean head, the most likely implication is that since a shrimp's head is already unclean, such a son-in-law would have no qualms about groveling in the dirt and putting his head to the floor in apology.[xix]

Bigger baddies (MS:29)

Master Mugwort was traveling by a water route when he caught sight of a tiny shrine decorated in particularly dignified manner. In front of the shrine ran a small channel. Master Mugwort watched as a passerby walked up to the channel's edge but was unable to ford it. The man's eyes fell on the contents of the shrine, and all of a sudden, he grabbed the idol of a Great King, lay it across the channel, walked over it, and went on his way![43]

Along came another man. Seeing the sorry state of the idol, he sighed more than once and said, "To think that even a divine idol could be treated with such contempt!" He stood it back up, and used his own clothes to wipe it down. Then he put it back onto its empty stand, bowed a few times, and left.

After a few moments, Master Mugwort heard one of the little minions in the shrine mutter, "Great King, the position you hold here is that of a god. Normally, you enjoy all manner of sacrifices from everyone in the neighborhood, yet here comes some imbecile who humiliates you! How about setting a curse to serve up his just desserts?"

王曰：「然則，禍當行於後來者。」小鬼又曰：「前人以履大王，辱莫甚焉，而不行禍。後來之人，敬大王者，反禍之。何也？」王曰：「前人已不信矣。又安敢禍之！」艾子曰：「真是鬼怕惡人也！」

[MS:30]

艾子有從禽之僻，畜一獵犬，甚能搏兔。艾子每出，必牽犬以自隨。凡獲兔，必出其心肝以與之食，莫不飫足。故凡獲一兔，犬必搖尾以視艾子，自喜而待其飼也。

一日，出獵。偶兔少而犬饑已甚。望草中二兔躍出，鷹翔而擊之。兔狡，翻覆之際，而犬已至。乃誤中其鷹，斃焉。而兔已走矣。艾子忽遽將死鷹在手。歎恨之次，犬亦如前搖尾而自喜，顧艾子以待食。艾子乃顧犬而罵曰：「這神狗猶自道我是裏。」

[MS:31]

艾子出遊，見一嫗白髮而衣衰纍之服，哭甚哀。

---

44 This scenario is replayed to a different effect in *At the foot of Mount Tai* (OS:9).
45 See *Dogs to the slaughter* (FS:14) for a good point of comparison.
46 She is wearing ritual attire worn for a specified period of filial mourning.

Said the King, "If I curse anybody, it'll be that second guy."

Said the minion, "The first guy stamped all over you—a humiliation for the Great King, yet you did not curse him. Meanwhile, the second guy treated the Great King with reverence, yet you curse him! Why?"

Said the King, "The first one clearly wasn't a believer. How would I even go about cursing him?"

Master Mugwort said, "Turns out it's true that 'Even demons fear bigger baddies!'"[44]

Master Mugwort takes his dog on a hunt (MS:30)

One of Master Mugwort's hobbies was hunting. He kept a hunting dog that had a special talent for catching rabbits. Whenever he set out on a hunt, Master Mugwort was sure to take the dog along with him. Each time it caught a rabbit, he would slice out the rabbit's innards and feed them to the dog, who never went hungry on a hunt. Thus trained, whenever the dog caught a rabbit, it would look to Master Mugwort and wag its tail, brimming with glee as it awaited its treat.

One day, they went out on a hunt. It so happened that there were very few rabbits about that day, and the dog was by this point incredibly hungry. In the distance, they caught sight of two rabbits hopping about in the undergrowth. Master Mugwort's hawk swooped down to strike, but this rabbit was a tough one, and the pair began to tussle. By that time, the dog had arrived on the scene and pounced on the hawk by mistake. The hawk was killed, and the rabbit got away.

Master Mugwort hurried over as quickly as he could, took the dead hawk into his hands and heaved several resentful sighs. But to his surprise, just as always, the dog stood there wagging his tail, looking gleefully at Master Mugwort in anticipation of a treat. Master Mugwort looked back at the dog and cursed it, "This blasted dog still thinks he's in the right!"

The analogy is likely with officials in receipt of a salary from the state. Here the official's overzealous and competitive attempts to meet his assigned target result in catastrophe—perhaps even the loss of a talented colleague. Yet, oblivious to the state in which he has left matters, back he comes to seek reward and approval, as if the disaster he has caused is a suitable replacement for the task originally assigned.[45]

Master Mugwort meets an old woman in mourning (MS:31)

When Master Mugwort was out on his travels, he saw a white-haired old woman in a tattered mourning garb, wailing as though inconsolably grief-stricken.[46]

　　艾子謂曰：「嫗何哭而若此之哀也？」嫗曰：「吾哭夫也。」艾子曰：「嫗自高年而始哭夫。不識夫誰也？」曰：「彭祖也。」艾子曰：「彭祖壽八百而死，固不為短，可以無恨。」嫗曰：「吾夫壽八百，誠無恨。然又有壽九百而不死者，豈不恨邪！」

[MS:32]

艾子之鄰，皆齊之鄙人也。聞一人相謂曰：「吾與齊之公卿，皆人，而稟三才之靈者。何彼有智，而我無智？」一曰：「彼日食肉，所以有智。我平日食糲糲，故少智也。」其問者曰：「吾適有糴粟錢數千，姑與汝日食肉試之。」數日，復又聞彼二人相謂曰：「吾自食肉後，心識明達，觸事有智。不徒有智，又能窮理。」其一曰：「吾觀人腳面前出甚便。若後出，豈不為繼來者所踐？」其一曰：「吾亦見人鼻竅，向下甚利。若向上，豈不為天雨注之乎？」

Master Mugwort said to the old woman, "Old dear, for whom are you wailing so mournfully?"

"I wail for my husband," said the old woman.

"Old dear, you would seem to have made it to a grand old age before having to cry over your husband's passing. Who might your husband be?"

"Ancestor Peng."

Said Master Mugwort, "Well, Ancestor Peng lived a long life of eight hundred years, after all. One could hardly call that untimely! It is not to be begrudged."

Said the old woman, "It's true my husband's eight hundred years are nothing to lament. But how can I help but feel sorry, when others have made it to nine!"

Ancestor Peng (*Peng zu*) was a legendary figure, chiefly remembered for living to an advanced old age. He was considered important in Daoist practice for his vital life spirit, and attained an additional reputation for virility and sexual prowess.

Master Mugwort's next-door neighbors (MS:32)

Master Mugwort's next-door neighbors were two of the biggest philistines in the whole of Qi. Once, he heard them talking between themselves: "The noblemen and ministers of this land are people just like us, right? But they know about all the matters of Heaven, Earth, and Mankind. How come they're so wise and we're not?"

Said the other, "They get to eat meat every day—that'll be where all that wisdom comes from. Meanwhile, we spend our days eating rough grain, and don't know much of anything."

The first one said, "As it happens, I've just sold some millet for several thousand in cash. How about we test it out by eating a daily portion of meat?"

A few days later, Master Mugwort heard the pair discussing how as soon as the meat experiment began, their mind's eye had become enlightened and insightful, with wisdom to dish out on every matter under the sun. In fact, not only had they become wise, but had even been endowed with a thorough grasp on the logic that underlay worldly phenomena.

Said the first, "I looked at someone's feet and realized the way they point forwards is in fact an extreme advantage. Were they to point backwards, they'd be sure to get trodden on by the guy walking behind."

Said the second, "Likewise, I looked at someone's nose and realized that the way nostrils open downwards is in fact of the utmost benefit. Were they to open upwards, they'd be sure to fill up with rainwater."

二人相稱其智。艾子歎曰:「肉食者,其智若此。」

[MS:33]

艾子病熱,稍昏,夢中神游陰府。見閻羅王升殿治事。有數鬼擡一人至。一吏前白之曰:「此人在世,唯務持人陰事,恐取財物。雖無過者,一巧造端以誘陷之,然後摘使準法,合以五百億萬斤柴,於鑊湯中煮訖放。」王可之。令付獄。有一牛頭捽執之而去。其人私謂牛頭曰:「君何人也?」曰:「吾鑊湯獄主也。獄之事,皆可主之。」

The two men applauded one another on their newfound insight. Master Mugwort sighed and remarked, "Precisely the kind of wisdom we expect from the meat-eaters."

Master Mugwort's dry remark here is not so much aimed at the two neighbors, but at the "wise" people they are attempting to imitate. In times when only the upper echelons of society could afford to eat meat on a regular basis, the term "eating meat" (*shirou* 食肉) came to be an epithet for men of high station and the state salary that accompanied it, such as enfeoffed noblemen or high-ranking ministers, who, as Mugwort observes, were wont to deploy just such "wisdom" and "insight" in their policy-making.

Leopard-skin loincloths (MS:33)

King Yama is one of the Ten Kings of Buddhist purgatory. Particularly prominent in art and literature, he is depicted as a magistrate whose job is to preside over the purgatorial court at which the recently deceased are judged for their sins. As we shall see in the following episode, one of his main roles is to determine the appropriate degree of purgatorial torture. Across East Asia, past and present, there is a ritual practice of burning real items or joss paper representations of money and other objects. The burning sends them to the other world and is intended to equip deceased relatives with all they may need in the afterlife. For another Yama episode, see *King Yama interrogates a former prime minister* (MS:39).

Master Mugwort was sick with a fever, and drifted in and out of consciousness. In a dreamlike state, his spirit traveled to the Netherworld, where he watched as King Yama conducted business in his courtroom.

Several demons arrived, dragging a man in with them. A clerk stepped forth to announce the accused: "During his lifetime, this man's sole pursuit was taking advantage of other people's secret desires to blackmail them out of money and property. Even those who had previously done no wrong were lured into his devious schemes and traps. The corresponding torture protocol is being boiled in a cauldron for the time it takes to burn up five hundred billion catties of firewood, before being sent on his way."

Yama indicated his approval, and ordered the man be consigned to the correct section of purgatory. A demon with the head of an ox seized the man and pulled him away.

"And who might you be, my good sir?" muttered the man discreetly to the Oxhead.

"I am Head of the Department of Boiling Cauldrons," replied the Oxhead. "I'm in charge of overseeing all aspects of this section of Purgatory."

其人又曰：「既為獄主，固首主也。而豹皮裩若此之弊！」
其鬼曰：「冥中無此皮。若陽人焚化方得。而吾名不顯於人
間，故無焚貺者。」其人又曰：「某之外氏，獵徒也，家常
有此皮。若蒙獄主見憫，少減柴數，得還，則焚化十皮為獄
主作裩。」其鬼喜曰：「為汝去億萬二字，以欺其徒，則汝
得速還，兼免沸煮之苦三之二也。」於是又入鑊煮之。其牛
頭者，時來相問。小鬼見如此，必欲庇之，亦不敢令火熾，
遂報柴足。既出鑊，束帶將行。牛頭曰：「勿忘皮也。其人
乃回顧曰：「有詩一首，奉贈。云：『牛頭獄主要知聞，權在
閻王不在君；減刻官柴猶自可，更求枉法豹皮裩。』」牛頭
大怒，又入鑊湯，益薪煮之。艾子既寤，語於徒曰：「須信
口是禍之門也。」

[MS:34]
艾子好為詩。一日，行齊魏間，宿逆旅。夜聞鄰房人言曰：

"If you're Section Head, then you're the top dog!" exclaimed the man. "And yet I notice that leopard-skin loincloth of yours is near falling to pieces."

"We don't have skins like this the Netherworld," sighed the Oxhead. "We can only get hold of them if someone from the human world burns them as an offering. Too bad my name isn't widely known among the living. I've got nobody to burn them for me."

"Why, my mother's family are hunters!" cried the man. "We always have a bunch of skins like that lying around at home. Say, with your authority as Section Head, if you would be so kind as to take pity on me and reduce the amount of firewood a teensy bit, then when I am granted my return, I shall burn ten whole skins to clothe the Section Head's loins."

The Oxhead was delighted. "I shall erase the words 'hundred' and 'billion' for you—that'll dupe the underlings. With that you'll be in and out in no time, and the discomfort of getting boiled will drop by two thirds to boot."

And so he put him in the cauldron and began the boiling process. The Oxhead dropped by periodically to check up on him, and noticing this, the minions knew that their boss intended for them to go easy on this one, and dared not so much as let the fire get going before reporting that the firewood quota had been reached. Once the man was back out of the cauldron, had done up his belt and was about to leave, the Oxhead reminded him, "Don't forget about the skins."

The man looked back at the Oxhead and said, "I've composed a poem especially for you:

> The Netherworld's home to an Ox
> Who's mistaken himself for the boss!
> He expunged my fate
> For a wardrobe update
> But the king round here's Yama. His loss![xx]

The Oxhead was furious. He dumped the man back into the cauldron with his pitchfork, shoveled on the firewood, and boiled him.

When Master Mugwort regained consciousness he said to his disciples, "They say the mouth is the gateway to trouble—you'd better believe it!"

Master Mugwort's love of poetry (MS:34)

Master Mugwort enjoyed composing *shi* poems.[xxi] One day, he was lodging at an inn somewhere between Qi and Wei, when during the night, he heard a voice coming from the neighboring room, which said,

「一首也。」少間曰:「又一首也。」比曉,六七首。艾子
其必詩人清夜吟詠。兼愛其敏思。淩晨,冠帶候謁。少頃,
一人出,乃商賈也。危羸若有疾者。艾子深感之。豈有是
人而能詩乎?抑又不可臆度。遂問曰:「聞足下篇什甚多,
敢乞一覽。」其人曰:「某負販也,安知詩為何物?」再三
拒之。艾子曰:「昨夜聞君房中自鳴曰:『一首也』,須臾,
又曰:「一首也」,豈非詩乎?」其人笑言:「君誤矣。昨
日每腹疾暴下。夜黑,尋紙不及。因污其手。疾勢不止,
殆六七污手,其言曰非詩也。」艾子有慚色。門人因戲之
曰:「先生求騷雅,乃是大儒。」

[MS:35]

艾子一日晨出,見齊之相府門前有數十人,皆貧窶之甚,人
相聚而立。因問之曰:「汝何者而集於此?」其人曰:「吾皆
齊之貧民,以少業自營,亦終歲不乏。今有至冤,欲訴於丞
相辨之。」

"One *shi*." After a short while the voice came again: "And another *shi*." By daybreak, this had happened six or seven times. Master Mugwort concluded that the guest next door must be a poet, composing verses in the depths of the night. With great admiration for the man's speed of composition, the following morning he put on formal attire and went to wait for the poet to come out of his room.

Before long, a man emerged, dressed like a merchant. He seemed gaunt and weak, as if unwell. Master Mugwort felt a deep pang of sympathy at the sight of him. How could a man endowed with such poetic talents have ended up in this state? Unable to fathom it, he said to the man, "Last night I overheard your honorable self composing a great many verses. I humbly entreat you to allow me a glimpse of your work!"

"Me? I am but a peddler! What could I possibly know about poetry?" protested the man, and he proceeded to rebuff Master Mugwort's pleas several times.

"Last night I heard you in your room muttering to yourself, saying 'One *shi*.' Then after a while you said, 'And another *shi*.'" said Master Mugwort. "You're telling me that wasn't about poems?"

The man laughed and said, "Good sir, you are mistaken. You see, I have a stomach ailment, and yesterday the diarrhea was explosive! I couldn't find any paper in the dark and had to use my hand. It didn't let up until I had dirtied my hands six or seven times. I was talking about shit, not *shi*!" Master Mugwort was visibly mortified.[xxii]

His disciples later teased him about this, saying, "Master, your quest for refined poetry is that of a great scholar!"[xxiii]

Master Mugwort sees a crowd at the prime ministerial residence (MS:35)

The next episode concerns two kinds of printed images: the "Rain-Dragon" and the "Barbarian-Pointing-at-the-Sun." The former was put on display in hope of rain, while the latter was displayed when clear weather was desired.

When Master Mugwort headed out one morning, he saw several dozen people in front of the gates to the residence of the Prime Minister of Qi. Clearly poverty-stricken, they were standing together in a crowd.

Master Mugwort asked one of them, "Why have you all assembled here?"

One answered, "We are the poor of Qi. We run a small business and we manage on our own. Normally, that ensures we want for nothing all year long. But recently we have suffered an injustice! We're here to argue our case before the Prime Minister himself."

艾子曰：「相府非辨訟之所。當詣士師也。」其人曰：「事由丞相，非士師可辨。」艾子曰：「然則何事也？」其人曰：「吾所業乃印雨龍與指日鸞也。今丞相為政數年，率春及夏旱。僕印賣求雨龍。纔秋至冬，多雨潦，即賣指日鸞。吾獲利以足衣食。皆前半年，取通債印造。及期無不售者。却去年冬，係大雪，接春，又陰晦，或雨，泥濘牛馬皮下，令人家求晴。吾數家，但習常年先印下求雨龍。唯一人有秋時剩下指日鸞，遂專其利。豈不為至冤乎？」艾子曰：「汝印者龍，當秋却售也。此乃丞相，恐人道變理手段，年年一般，且要倒過耳。」

[MS:36]

秦既併滅六國，專有天下，罷侯置守。艾子當是時，與秦之相有舊。喜以趣之，欲求一佳郡守。

47　For an overview of this scheme, see Miyazaki 1967, 82–86.

48　Chu, Wei, Hann, Zhao, Qi and Yan. On the historical reality, see Li 2022.

49　We can assume readers would have known that the Prime Minister at this momentous point in history was Li Si, famous for his emphasis on meritocratic selection criteria, which would indirectly prove his downfall. The name may not have been pinned down deliberately so as not to void the dual function of satire of later Prime Minister(s).

Said Master Mugwort, "The Prime Minister's residence is not the place to contest a lawsuit. You should redirect your concerns to the Chief Judge."

Said the man, "But the complaint originates with the Prime Minister himself! It's not something that the Chief Judge can adjudicate."

Said Master Mugwort, "Then what kind of issue is it?"

The man said, "Our trade is Rain-Dragon and Barbarian-Pointing-at-the-Sun prints. In the years since the Prime Minister has been in office, the weather has been dry from spring to summer without exception. So I print Rain-Dragons to sell. And from autumn to winter there are frequent rains and floods, so I sell Barbarian-Pointing-at-the-Sun prints. With that, I can make just enough to put food on the table and clothes on my back. In both cases, I take out one of his loans for the printing costs half a year in advance—by the end of the loan period, I've always sold out! But last year, there was heavy snow in the winter, which lasted right up until the spring. The skies were gloomy. Sometimes the rain and mud soaked the livestock right down to their skin. It made people long for clear weather. All of us here did what we do every year and printed the Rain-Dragons. Only one guy had some leftover Barbarians from the autumn, and he made the most of his monopoly by gouging the price! Isn't that just the worst injustice?"

Master Mugwort said, "Well, you've got Rain-Dragons, and you'll be able to sell them come autumn. What we are looking at here is one of our Prime Minister's strategies for the good of humanity. Seeing how each year has always been the same, he wanted to shake things up a bit."

A possible satire of the "green sprouts" (*qingmiao* 青苗) farming loans initiated by Wang Anshi, or their later iterations. One of the first of the New Policies to be implemented, this meant the introduction of a governmental lending scheme processed by local granaries which could be taken out and repaid in spring and autumn respectively.[47] Originally intended to reduce farmers' dependency on unregulated loans from landowners, the scheme came under fire for its inflexible timeframe and blanket implementation, which did not accommodate for events like unpredictable weather.

Master Mugwort visits the Prime Minister of Qin (MS:36)

Once the State of Qin had vanquished and annexed the other six major states to reach sole domination over All Under Heaven, it did away with the fiefdoms and instead installed regional governors.[48]

As it happened, Master Mugwort had a long-standing friendship with the Prime Minister of Qin at the time.[49] Rejoicing in his luck, Master Mugwort made haste to visit him in the hope of getting his hands on a

秦相見艾子，甚篤故情。日延飲食，皆玉醴珍饌。數日，以
情白之。相欣然謂曰：「細事，可必副所欲。」又數日，乃
曰：「欲以一寸原。」艾子曰：「吾見丞相望之。然又日享甘
旨，必謂甚有籌畫。元來只有生得耀州知白。」

[MS:37]

齊之士子，相尚裹烏紗帽，長其頂，短其簷，直其勢，以其
紗相粘為之。虛粘奇帽，設肆相接。其一家自榜其門曰當
鋪，每頂只賣八百文。以其廉，人日雍門。以是多愆期。一
日，艾子方坐其肆，見一士子與其肆主語：「吾先數日約要
帽，反失期五七日，尚未得。必是為他人皆賣九百文，爾獨
卑於價以欺吾也。」呶呶久之。艾子因曰：「秀才但勿喧。
只管將八百文錢與他，須要九百底帽子。」

[MS:38]

齊有二老臣，皆累朝宿儒大老，社稷倚重。一曰冢相，凡國
之重事，乃關預焉。一日，齊王下令遷都。有一寶鍾，重
五千斤，計人力須五百人可扛。

50　Or "The Functionless Prefect of Yaozhou," the character *yao* 耀 carrying the meanings "glory" and "bewildered."

51　For more hats, see *The Jade Emperor's birthday party* (OS:11).

52　"Great Altars to the Gods of Earth and Grain" refers to the State.

decent fiefdom. The Prime Minister duly met with Master Mugwort and reminisced over old memories with sincere tenderness. Day after day, he invited Master Mugwort for dinner and drinks, each time serving up exquisite wines and rare delicacies.

After a few days of this, Master Mugwort confessed that he was hoping for a governorship. "That's nothing," replied the Prime Minister cheerfully. "Your wish is my command."

But then a few days later, he announced to him, "I've gotten you an inch of land."

Master Mugwort said, "I came to you with great expectations, and even got to eat delicious food for days on end. I thought you must have grand plans for me, but in the end all you came up with was 'Functionless Prefect of Honorary County!'"[50]

The scholars of Qi and their black gauze hats (MS:37)

The scholars of Qi set great store by their black gauze hats. The hats had a tall crest with a short rim and rigid body, all bound together by gauze. Thus they were known as Extraordinary Glueless Hats, and the streets were lined with purveyors of such wares. There was one store with a board at the door which read "Pawn Shop." There, each hat sold for just eight hundred coins. That was good value, so there were crowds of customers at the gates every day. But because of this, production was often behind schedule.

One day, Master Mugwort had just been seated inside this establishment when he saw a scholar talking at the store owner, saying, "I ordered a hat days ago, but it's late by nearly a week now, and I still haven't got my hat! You must've sold it to some other guy for nine hundred coins and just made up that lower price to cheat me." He railed on like this for some time.

Master Mugwort said, "No need to make a racket, dear scholar. You're the one who gave him eight hundred coins and asked for a hat worth nine hundred!"[51]

The old ministers of Qi (MS:38)

In Qi, there were two old ministers. These much-esteemed elders were wizened scholars who had served under several consecutive courts, upon whom the Great Altars to the Gods of Earth and Grain depended for their highly valued input.[52] One was known as the First Minister, and he was given a say in all matters of consequence in the land.

One day, the King of Qi issued an edict ordering that the capital be moved to a different city. In the process, there arose the matter of a precious royal bell weighing five thousand catties. It was estimated that the bell would require the combined strength of five hundred men

時齊無人。有司計無所出。乃白亞相。久亦無語。徐曰：
「嘻！此事亞相何不能了也！」於是令有司曰：「一鍾之
重，五百人可扛。人忽，均鑿作五百段，用一人，五百日扛
之。」有司欣然承命。艾子適見之，乃曰：「冢宰奇畫，人
固不及。只是搬到彼，莫却費錭鏴也無？」

[MS:39]

齊宣王時，人有死而生，能言陰府間言。乃云：「方在陰府
之（時），見閻羅王詰責一貴人，曰：『汝何得罪之多也？』
因問曰：『何人也？』『魯正卿季氏也。』其貴人再三不服。
曰：『無罪。』閻王曰：『某年，齊人侵境，汝只遣萬人往應
之。皆曰：多寡不敵，必無功。豈徒無功，必枉害人之命。
汝復而不從。是以齊兵衆，萬人皆死。又某年某日饑，汝蔽
君之聰明而不言，遂不發廩，因此死數萬人。又汝為人相，
職在燮理陰陽。汝為政乖戾，多致水旱，歲之民被其害。此
皆汝之罪也。』其貴人叩頭乃服。王曰：『可付阿鼻獄。』
乃有牛頭人數輩，執之而去。」

to transport, a level of manpower that Qi could not spare at that particular moment.

The underlings simply could not think of a way around it, and confessed this to the Second Minister, who dwelt upon the matter at length before the First Minister finally exclaimed, "Pfft, what about this is so tricky for you, Second Minister?"[xxiv] He instructed the underlings: "So, the weight of one bell takes five hundred men to carry. I say cut it into five hundred equally-sized pieces! That way it'll only take one man five hundred days." And the underlings set the order in motion with great zeal.

As Master Mugwort watched this unfold, he remarked, "To be sure, the marvelous schemes of the First Minister are beyond the reach of mere mortals! One thing, though. Once you've moved it over, who's going to pay to put it back together again?"

King Yama interrogates a former Prime Minister (MS:39)

In the time of King Xuan of Qi, there was a man who died and came back to life, and so could tell stories about what he had seen in the Netherworld. He said:

Back in the Netherworld, I watched King Yama interrogating a nobleman.[xxv] Muttering 'How did you manage to rack up *this* many sins?' he began the interrogation: 'So, who are you?'

'I am Ji, Prime Minister of the State of Lu,' replied the nobleman, and then refused to confess several times over. 'I have no sins to my name!'

King Yama said, 'One year, when Qi breached Lu's borders, you sent only ten thousand men in response to the invasion. Everyone said that so few soldiers would be no match for the enemy and the expedition would never succeed. Not only that, but the lives of the men would be lost in vain. But you paid no heed to the repeated calls, and as a result those ten thousand men were killed by the massive Qi army. On top of this, another year there was a famine, but you deliberately concealed this from your ruler and said nothing. Consequently, he did not open up the emergency granaries and several tens of thousands starved to death. As Prime Minister, your duty was to take care of the affairs of state, but thanks to your erratic policies, there were many floods and droughts that wreaked havoc among the common folk, year after year. All of that was your fault.'

The nobleman kowtowed and confessed his guilt. King Yama said, 'This one deserves Avīci, the deepest level of hell.' With that, a gang of Oxheads escorted him away.

　　艾子聞之，太息不已。門人問曰：「先生與季氏有舊
邪？何歎也？」艾子曰：「我非歎季氏也，蓋歎閻羅王也。」
門人曰：「何謂也？」曰：「自此安得獄空邪？」

After hearing this, Master Mugwort could not hold back his sighs.

One of his disciples asked him, "Why do you sigh so, Master? Was Mr. Ji a friend of yours?"

"No, it's not about Mr. Ji," replied Master Mugwort. "I suppose I am sighing for King Yama."

"What do you mean?"

"Well, if it's cases like that, the poor King is going to have his hands full."

King Yama spends eternity passing judgement over the dead in Buddhist purgatory. Looking at the sorry state of governance in the living world and knowing the endless flow of evil prime ministers that has yet to pass before Yama's desk—from Warring States right down to the Song—our protagonist sighs with the empathy of a fellow bureaucrat.

艾子後語

[序]

世皆知艾子為坡翁戲筆，而不知其有為作也。觀其問蟹、問
米、乘驢之說，則以譏父子；獮瘃、雨龍、移鐘之說，則以
譏時相。即其意指，其殆為王氏作乎？坡翁平日好以言語文
章規切時政，若此亦其一也。余幼有謔癖，有所得必志之。
歲丙子，遊金陵，客居無聊，因取其尤雅者，纂而成編，以
附於坡翁之後，直用為戲耳，若謂其意有所寓者，則吾豈
敢！

是歲九月望，長洲陸灼識。

[FS:1]

齊大夫邴石父謀叛，宣王誅之。欲滅其族。邴之族大以蕃，
聚而謀曰：「他人之言王必不內，惟艾先生辨而有寵，盍往
祈焉？」舉族拜於艾子之庭，涕泗以請。艾子笑曰：「是不
難。諸公但具一繩來，立可免禍。」

---

1   The first episodes mentioned by Lu Cai are MS:2 and MS:26. As for the third, there does
not seem to be an episode about donkey-riding in the received versions. Perhaps it is a
mistake for "feeding the donkey" (MS:3), though there are indeed humorous anecdotes
about Wang Anshi's donkey-riding habits during his retirement. "Fathers and sons" is
often a metaphor for "rulers and ministers," and the final three episodes mentioned are
MS:22, MS:35, MS:38.

The Ming Sequels
Further Sayings of Master Mugwort

Preface

The whole world knows *Master Mugwort* to be the Slope Codger's playful brushstrokes, yet it is not known why he wrote it. The "Asking about crabs," "Asking about rice," and "Riding a donkey" stories appear to be mocking fathers and sons, while the "Monoceros," "Rain-Dragons," and "Moving the clock" stories mock the Prime Minister of the day.[1] Given these intended targets, isn't the work most likely written about Mr. Wang?[2] The Slope Codger was generally fond of using his words and writings to remonstrate against the governance of the time. This work seems to be another instance.

For my part, I have had a weakness for jokes since I was young, and whenever I come across one I am sure to make a note of it. In 1516 I was on a trip to Jinling and there was nothing to do at the guest lodgings; so I selected those of superior tastefulness and collated them into a book, to be appended after the one by the Slope Codger. It is to be used merely for fun and nothing more. And if it be said that there are hidden meanings lodged inside—well, how could I dare?

Signed, Lu Zhuo of Changzhou, that same year,
at the start of the ninth month.

Three feet of rope (FS:1)

In the State of Qi, the grandee Zhu Shifu had been caught plotting a coup.[xxvi] King Xuan put him to death and was about to extinguish his entire clan. The Zhu clan was large and prosperous, and they gathered together to hatch a plan: "The King never listens to what other people say. The only one who can persuade him onto a different course while remaining in good favor is Venerable Sir Mugwort. We should go entreat him to intervene."

The entire clan headed over to Master Mugwort's front courtyard, where they bowed before him, begging his assistance as they wept and sniveled.

Master Mugwort chuckled. "No trouble at all, gentlemen. Kindly just procure a length of rope and bring it here. With that, I'll be able to secure you a pardon from this unfortunate predicament in no time."

---

2 Wang Anshi. See "The Northern Song political context" section above.

郗氏以為戲言，亦不敢詰。退而索綯以餽。艾子懷其三尺以
見王，曰：「郗石父包藏禍心，王肆諸市，當矣。然為之者
石父一人耳。其宗族何辜，而王欲盡殲之？無乃非仁君之用
心乎！」宣王曰：「此非寡人意也，先王之律有明訓也。政
典曰：『與叛同宗者殺無赦。』是以寡人不敢曲宥以傷先王
之法。」艾子頓首曰：「臣亦知王之不得已也。竊有一說焉：
往年公子巫以邯鄲降秦，非大王之母弟乎？以是而言，大王
亦叛臣之族，理合隨坐。臣有短繩三尺，敢獻於下執事，請
大王即日引決，勿惜一身而傷先王之法。」王笑而起曰：「先
生且休！寡人赦之矣。」

3   Capital punishment as a deterrent to others.
4   The sage rulers of antiquity.
5   As related in chapter 86 of *Records of the Historian* (Nienhauser, 1994–, vol. VII, 593–630;
    Records of the Historian 86.2526–2536).

The Zhus thought this must be some kind of joke, but dared not inquire further. They retreated to look for a roll of rope and duly presented it to Master Mugwort.

Indeed, Master Mugwort appeared at his next audience with three feet of it bundled up in his arms. He faced King Xuan and proclaimed, "Zhu Shifu harbored wicked intentions, so it was only fitting that my King 'exposed his corpse in the marketplace,' so to speak.[3] However, the perpetrator was Shifu and Shifu alone. What are his ancestors and descendants guilty of, to merit my King's desire to exterminate every last one of them? If they are indeed innocent, then this is not the attitude of a humane ruler!"

"This was not Our own idea!" protested King Xuan. "It is a clear instruction from the Former Kings themselves.[4] Their statutes of governance state that, 'As to those who share the bloodline of a rebel, kill them, sparing none.' This being so, your King does not venture to bend the rule for the Zhus' sake in violation of the laws of the Former Kings."

Master Mugwort descended into a kowtow and said, "Your servant understands that his King's hands are tied in the matter. Unworthy as I am, I have a suggestion of my own. In years past, Prince Wu surrendered Handan to Qin. Was he not my Great King's brother, born of the same womb? In light of this, our Great King is also the clansman of a rebel minister, and it stands to reason that He be punished accordingly. Your servant happens to have a short length of rope right here with him, which he presumes to offer to you with which to do the deed. Great King, I beseech you! End it on this very day—do not cherish this body of yours in dereliction of an order from the Former Kings!"

The King laughed, rose to his feet and said, "Enough for now, Venerable Sir. We shall pardon them."[xxvii]

Unfinished business (FS:2)

At the eve of the Warring States period, when the small number of states that remained looked on as Qin slowly but surely engulfed the world surrounding them, the State of Yan's heir apparent, Dan, made a last-ditch attempt to slow the advance, by cajoling a man named Jing Ke to make an assassination attempt against the future First Emperor. Jing Ke persuaded a runaway Qin general Fan Yuqi to part with his head, who, prepared to support the cause at any cost, cut his own throat on the spot. The promise of Fan Yuqi's head enabled Jing Ke to secure an audience at the Qin court. Jing Ke grabbed the king and raised his poisoned dagger, but the king managed to prize himself from his clutches. Eventually, a group of armed guards arrived on the scene and hacked Jing Ke to pieces. Fan Yuqi had given his head in vain, while Yan was annexed in a matter of years.[5]

[FS:2]

艾子夜夢游上清朝天帝。見一人戎服帶劍而失其首，頸血淋漓，手持奏章而進。其辭曰：「訴寃臣秦國樊於期，得罪亡奔在燕。有不了事。衛荊軻借去頭顱一箇，至今本利未還；燕太子丹為証見，伏乞追給！」天帝覽之，蹙額而言曰：「渠自家手脚也沒討處，何暇還你頭顱？」於期乃退。艾子亦覺。

[FS:3]

艾子在齊居孟嘗君門下者三年。孟嘗君禮為上客。既而自齊反乎魯，與季孫氏遇。季孫曰：「先生久於齊，齊之賢者為誰？」艾子曰：「無如孟嘗君。」季孫曰：「何德而謂賢？」艾子曰：「食客三千，衣廩無倦色，不賢而能之乎？」季孫曰：「嘻！先生欺余哉！三千客余家亦有之，豈獨田文？」艾子不覺斂容而起，謝曰：「公亦魯之賢者也！翌日敢造門下求觀三千客。」季孫曰：「諾。」

6   Shangqing 上清, Daoist heavenly realm of the highest order.
7   Nienhauser 1994–, vol. VII, 345–366; *Records of the Historian* 74.2343–2363.
8   There were several notable Jisuns associated with the State of Lu, especially during the Spring and Autumn period.

One night in his dreams, Master Mugwort traveled to the Realm of Supreme Purity to attend an audience with the Heavenly Emperor.[6] There entered a man dressed for battle, with a sword but no head. As the blood dribbled from his severed neck, he submitted a formal accusation to the Emperor that read: "I, the aggrieved, am Fan Yuqi, originally of the State of Qin, but I offended its king and deserted to Yan. I have unfinished business. I loaned my head to Jing Ke of Wey, but to this very day he has returned neither capital nor interest! Crown Prince Dan of Yan can testify to it. I humbly request that Jing Ke be pursued on this matter."

The Heavenly Emperor glanced through the accusation, raised his eyebrows and said, "And how is the man supposed to find the time to give back your head when he's still looking for his own hands and feet?"

With that, Yuqi retired from court and Master Mugwort woke up.

Mr. Jisun's retinue (FS:3)

The name of Tian Wen, the Lord of Mengchang, is synonymous with his retinue of three thousand (see "China in the Warring States period" in the Introduction).[7] A kinsman of the Qi royal family and a key player in the politics and diplomacy of his day, stories of the Lord's life describe him as prescient with regard to the importance of keeping a retinue in the multi-state context and particularly open-armed when it came to swelling the ranks of his new retinue, even to the point of foolhardiness.

Master Mugwort had been in the State of Qi living as part of the Lord of Mengchang's retinue for three years. His Lordship granted him sumptuous treatment as one of his top retainers. Subsequently, he returned to Lu, where he ran into Mr. Jisun.[8]

Jisun said, "Venerable Sir, you were in Qi for quite some time. Pray, who are the worthy men around those parts?"

"None more than the Lord of Mengchang," replied Master Mugwort.

"And what virtues does the man possess to merit such a reputation?"

"He keeps a full three thousand under his patronage," replied Master Mugwort. "And he is tireless in ensuring they want for nothing. A man any less worthy could not manage it."

"Bah!" snorted Jisun. "The Venerable Sir surely deceives me. If three thousand retainers is all it takes, then even I've got that! Tian Wen isn't alone there."

At this reply, Master Mugwort's expression shifted into a more courteous one and he stood up to leave. "It would seem I am in the presence of a worthy man of Lu. In that case, I shall presume to drop by your residence tomorrow morning, where I expect to see three thousand men."

"That you shall," replied Jisun.

明旦，艾子衣冠齋潔而往。入其門，寂然也；升其堂，則無人焉。艾子疑之。意其必在別館也。良久，季孫出見。詰之曰：「客安在？」季孫悵然曰：「先生來何暮？三千客各自歸家喫飯去矣。」艾子胡盧而退。

[FS:4]

艾子講道於嬴博之間，齊魯之士從之者數十百人。一日，講文王羑里之囚，偶赴宣王召，不及竟其說。一士怏怏返舍。其妻問之曰：「子日聞夫子之教，歸必欣然，今何不樂之甚？」士曰：「朝來聞夫子說周文王聖人也，今被其主殷紂囚於羑里。吾憐其無辜，是以深生愁惱。」妻欲寬其憂，姑慰之曰：「今雖見囚，久當放赦，豈必禁錮終身？」士嘆息曰：「不愁不放，只愁今夜在牢內難過活耳。」

---

9   To wash one's body and put on a clean set of clothes was considered a sign of respect
     and sincerity to the recipient of a visit.
10   Ying and Bo are two areas within the State of Qi, present-day Shandong province. See
     Map 2. "The Way" here likely indicates *Daoxue* 道學, likely in reference to the Cheng-
     Zhu branch of Confucianism (Matsueda 1970, 93).

At dawn the next day, Master Mugwort donned a fresh set of robes and set off to Mr. Jisun's residence.[9] Upon entering, however, he found it silent and empty. He ascended to the main hall, but there was not a soul in sight.

Finding this rather suspect, Master Mugwort figured that the retainers must be lodged in separate quarters. After quite some time, Jisun finally made his appearance.

"Where is your retinue, then?" demanded Master Mugwort.

"Why so late, Venerable Sir?" came the doleful response. "My three thousand men have all gone home to eat breakfast already!"

Master Mugwort scoffed and hit the road.[xxviii]

Master Mugwort gives a lecture (FS:4)

Master Mugwort was giving lectures on the Way between Ying and Bo, and they drew crowds of hundreds of scholars from Qi and Lu.[10] One day, he happened to receive urgent summons from King Xuan while in the middle of delivering a lecture on King Wen's imprisonment at Youli, and had to hurry off without finishing the talk.

One of the scholars in attendance headed back home distraught, so his wife said to him, "When you go to hear the Master's teachings during the daytime, you're sure to come back in an animated mood. So why do you seem so unhappy this time?"

"This morning the Master was talking about the sage King Wen of Zhou," replied the scholar. "As things stand, the King has been imprisoned in Youli by his ruler, Zhòu of Yin, and I find it so dreadful—the man is innocent![11] That's what's gotten me so upset."

Hoping to cheer him up a little, the scholar's wife consoled him by saying, "Well, he might be in prison for now, but after a while he'll be released. They surely can't lock him away for the rest of his life!"

The scholar sighed with feeling and said, "No, I'm not sad because I think he'll never get out. I just feel bad that he's spending a hard night in the slammer, that's all."

King Wen of Zhou was eventually released from his grueling stint behind bars, after which he set about gathering support for an ultimately successful attempt to overthrow King Zhòu, putting an end to the Shang dynasty. The practice of well-educated figures giving public lectures on Confucian topics was widespread in the Ming, particularly given the rise in the number of civil examination candidates. Here we find a slightly ambivalent glimpse of these lectures as an institution along with a subtle (yet not necessarily ill-spirited) jab at the quality of scholar they attracted.

11   Yin is an alternative name for the Shang dynasty (see Table of Dynasties).

[FS:5]

艾子遊於郊外，弟子通執二子從焉。渴甚，使執子乞漿於田舍。有老父映門觀書，執子揖而請。老父指卷中「真」字問曰：「識此字，餽汝漿。執子曰：「『真』字也。」父怒不與。執子返以告。艾子曰：「執也，未達；通也，當往。」通子見父，父如前示之。通子曰：「此『直八』兩字也。」父喜，出家釀之美者與之。艾子飲而甘之，曰：「通也，智哉！使復如執之認真，一勺水吾將不得吞矣。」

[FS:6]

艾子有孫年十許，慵劣不學，每加榎楚而不悛。其子僅有是兒，恒恐兒之不勝杖而死也，責必涕泣以請。艾子怒曰：「吾為若教子不善邪？」杖之愈峻。其子無如之何。一旦雪作，孫搏雪而嬉。艾子見之，褫其衣使跪雪中，寒戰之色可掬。

---

12 The names of the disciples, Tong 通 and Zhi 執 stand for the pairs' signature character traits, respectively "unobstructed open-mindedness" and "inflexibly tethered to a way of doing something."

Truthfulness (FS:5)

Master Mugwort was traveling in the suburbs with two young disciples in tow named Outside-the-Box and Inside-the-Box.[12] He was getting very thirsty, so he sent Inside-the-Box to a farmhouse to ask for something to drink. Upon entry, he saw an old man with his back to the door, reading a book. Inside-the-Box clasped his hands to implore the man for some water. The old man pointed at the character for "truth" in the volume and told him, "If you know this character, I'll give you some water."

"It says 'truth,'" replied Inside-the-Box. The old man seemed irritated by this response and would not give him anything to drink.

The disciple dutifully returned to report what had happened to Master Mugwort, whose response was, "Inside, your insight is yet to reach the required level. Outside-the-Box! You go instead."

Outside-the-Box went to see the old man, who showed him the same character as before. "It's the two characters 'straight' and 'eight,'" said Outside-the-Box.

The old man was delighted to hear this and brought out one of his finest homemade wines.

Savoring the sweetness of the wine, Master Mugwort said, "How wise you are, Outside! If you had been as 'truthful' as Inside, I wouldn't have even gotten a spoonful of water!"

In premodern Chinese books, the text runs from top to bottom. Thus the character zhen 真 ("truth") does indeed resemble a zhi 直 ("straight") followed by a ba 八 ("eight"). Mugwort's remark at the end is a pun: "If you had been as serious (*renzhen* 認真) as Inside," but also literally "If you had recognized the character for 'truth' correctly like Inside did."

Master Mugwort's grandson (FS:6)

Master Mugwort had a grandson of around nine years of age. He was lazy and naughty and would not apply himself to his studies, behavior which did not improve even after he was punished with caning. Master Mugwort's son had only one male child, and he was afraid that the boy might die from the canings. So whenever he was scolded, the boy would always run crying and sniveling to his father.

Master Mugwort was angry at this state of affairs and said, "So my way of educating your child is no good, huh?" Then he would cane the boy even harder, and his son was helpless to interfere.

One morning after a snowfall, Master Mugwort's grandson went outside to play and roll snowballs. When Master Mugwort caught sight of this, he removed the child's upper garments and made him kneel in the snow. The boy was visibly shaking from the cold, but Master Mugwort's

其子不復敢言，亦脫其衣跪其旁。艾子驚問曰：「汝兒有罪，應受此罰。汝何與焉？」其子泣曰：「汝凍吾兒，吾亦凍汝兒。」艾子笑而釋之。

[FS:7]

趙有方士，好大言。艾子戲問之曰：「先生壽幾何？」方士啞然曰：「余亦忘之矣。憶童稺時與群兒往看宓羲畫八卦，見其蛇身人首，歸得驚癇，賴宓羲治以草頭藥治余得不死。女媧之世，天傾西北，地陷東南，余時居中央平穩之處，兩不能害。神農播厥穀，余已辟穀久矣，一粒不曾入口。蚩尤犯余以五兵，因舉一指擊傷其額，流血被面而遁。蒼氏子不識字，欲來求教。為其愚甚不屑也。慶都十四月而生堯，延余作湯餅會。舜為父母所虐，號泣于旻天。余手為拭淚，敦勉再三，遂以孝聞。

---

13 Fuxi is the mythological creator of the world, who is often credited as having invented the Eight Trigrams, used in geomancy and other forms of divination.

14 Nüwa is mythological figure credited with the creation of humans. When one of the pillars holding up the sky collapsed, causing the calamitous situation described here, she took pity on the humans and repaired it.

son did not dare speak out. Instead, he removed his own upper garments and knelt by the boy's side.

In surprise, Master Mugwort asked, "Your son is at fault and needs to be punished. But what have *you* done to deserve this punishment?"

Tearfully, Master Mugwort's son replied, "If you freeze my son to death, I'll freeze yours!"

Master Mugwort laughed and let them go.[xxix]

Master Mugwort teases an alchemist (FS:7)

There was an alchemist in the State of Zhao who was given to bragging. For sport, Master Mugwort asked him, "My learned senior, how long have you lived?"

"Even I've forgotten!" the alchemist snorted. "But I can remember going with a group of other kids to watch Fuxi write the Eight Trigrams as a child.[13] The shock of seeing him with the head of a man and the body of a snake gave me a seizure, and were it not for his remedy of medicinal herbs I would have died! In the time of Nüwa, the Heavens dropped towards the northwest, and the Earth slid towards the southwest.[14] But at the time I was living right at the stable point at the middle, and was thus harmed by neither. Until Shennong sowed the seeds to grow crops, I had undergone a lengthy fast, and not even a single grain had passed these lips of mine![15] One time, Chiyou came at me in battle with five weapons at once![16] But when I raised my pinky and poked him in the forehead, he bolted with blood streaming down his face. Once, a son from the Cang clan didn't know how to read and came to me for instruction. He was no quick learner, so it was a such a chore.[17] I remember when Qingdu was pregnant with the sage ruler Yao, the pregnancy took fourteen whole months and they had to keep postponing the celebratory noodle party![18] And when the sage ruler Shun was terrorized by his parents and cried out to the Heavens, I wiped his tears away with this very hand, then gave him a piece of my mind! That was

15 Shennong, the "Divine Farmer," a mythological ruler credited with the popularization of agricultural methods and tools.

16 Chiyou is a mythological figure often depicted as having many arms and legs, hence the five weapons here. He was the enemy of the Yellow Emperor and did battle with him at Zhuolu 涿鹿, the likely setting for the alchemist's encounter.

17 That is, Cang Jie, the mythological inventor of Chinese characters. This seems to be the point at which our alchemist inserts himself into the story: here, rather than coming up with the script himself, Cang Jie simply learns it from the alchemist.

18 Qingdu was a concubine of Emperor Ku, who was said to have given birth to Yao after an unusually long pregnancy (Standaert 2016, 169–225). The *tangbing hui*, here rendered "celebratory noodle party" was held a few days or months after the birth of a child.

禹治水經余門，勞而觴之，力辭不飲而去。孔甲贈余龍醢一
罍。余悞食之，于今口尚腥臭。成湯開一面之網以羅禽獸，
嘗面笑其不能忘情於野味。履癸強余牛飲不從，寘余炮烙之
刑，七晝夜而言笑自若，乃得釋去。姜家小兒釣得鮮魚，時
時相餉，餘以飼山中黃鶴。穆天子瑤池之宴，讓余首席。徐
偃稱兵，天子乘八駿而返。阿母留余終席。為飲桑落之酒過
多，醉倒不起。幸有董雙成、萼綠華兩箇丫頭，相扶歸舍。
一向沉醉至今，猶未全醒。不知今日世上是何甲子也？」

---

19   Following his father, mother, and brother's repeated attempts to kill him, Shun ran distraught into the fields and cried out to the heavens, but still bore his family no resentment.
Here the alchemist misrepresents why Shun was crying and takes credit for persuading
him onto a more filial course.

how he got his reputation for being so filial.[19] When Yu was off taming the floods, he passed by my gates. I invited him in for a drink to repay his labors, but he vigorously refused and kept on his way.[20] And once, Kong Jia bestowed a portion of dragon mince upon me, which I made the mistake of eating. My breath has stunk ever since![21] When Cheng Tang opened all but one side of the hunting net for the birds and beasts, I laughed at him for getting so emotionally attached to the wildlife.[22] Around then, Lü Gui forced me to join him in his wild drinking sessions. When I refused, he strapped me to one of his burning torture pillars. So I kept my cool and partied along for seven days and seven nights, and he finally let me go.[23] And when my buddy Jiang had caught himself a fresh'un, he would sometimes give some of it to me and feed the rest to the yellow cranes on the mountain.[24] Later on, King Mu let me sit at the top of the table at the Jasper Lake banquet, but before long Yan of Xu launched his army, at which point King Mu got up and headed back with his eight steeds.[25] But Ol' Mommy insisted I stay until the banquet finished, and I ended up on the floor after drinking too much of that 'mulberry aflutter' wine.[26] Thankfully those two lasses Perfectpair and Limeflower were around to help me back home, but to this very day that drunken haze has never quite worn off.[27] Who knows what year it is here on earth!"

20 The floods that Yu famously tamed broke out a few days after his wedding. Over the course of many years, Yu happened to pass by his home three times, but was too committed to his duties to stop.

21 Kong Jia was a famously superstitious ruler of the Xia dynasty. After one of his pet dragons died, the dragon-keeper minced its flesh and gifted it to him.

22 Cheng Tang, or Tang of Shang, was founder of the Shang dynasty. The story goes that he came across a hunter who had set up an inescapable four-sided net. Tang declared that the birds and beasts should at least be given a chance to escape, and took it upon himself to dismantle three sides of the net. This act of compassion is in fact supposed to have persuaded many to pledge allegiance to Tang in what turned out to be a successful rebellion against the tyrant ruler Lü Gui.

23 Lü Gui, or Jie of Xia, was the final ruler of the Xia dynasty, remembered for his orgies and excessively cruel punishments.

24 Jiang Ziya was the military strategist behind the overthrowing of the last Shang dynasty ruler. He was recruited by the (posthumously titled) King Wen of Zhou who came across him fishing without a hook.

25 King Mu was a Western Zhou ruler. His much fabled visit to the Jasper Lake, home of the Queen Mother of the West, a central figure in the Daoist pantheon, is recorded in the *Tradition of King Mu* (*Muyanzii zhuan* 穆天子傳). See Porter 1996. The army mention alludes to a raid on a Western Zhou capital by a southerly state.

26 *Sangluo jiu* 桑落酒, a renowned kind of wine.

27 Dong Shuangcheng ("Perfectpair") and E Lühua ("Lime[-green]flower") were two female Daoist immortals.

艾子唯唯而退。俄而趙王墮馬傷脇。醫云：「須千年血竭傅之。」乃差下令求血竭不可得。艾子言于王曰：「此有方士，不啻數千歲，殺取其血，其効當愈速矣。」王大喜，密使人執方士。將殺之。方士拜且泣曰：「昨者吾父母皆年五十，東鄰老姥携酒為壽，臣飲至醉，不覺言詞過度。實不曾活千歲，艾先生最善說謊，王其勿聽！」趙王乃叱而赦之。

[FS:8]

燕里季之妻美而蕩，私其鄰少年。季聞而思襲之，一旦伏而覘焉。見少年入室，而門扃矣。因起叩門，妻驚曰：「吾夫也，奈何？」少年顧問：「有牖乎？」妻曰：「此無牖。」「有竇乎？」妻曰：「此無竇。」「然則安出？」妻目壁間布囊曰：「是足矣。」少年乃入囊，懸之牀側曰：「問及，則紿以米也。」啓門內季。季遍室中求之不得，徐至牀側，其囊累然而見。舉之甚重。詰其妻曰：「是何物？」妻懼甚，囁嚅久之，不能答。而季屬聲呵問不已。

---

28 Medicinal "dragon's blood," in reality most often a reddish tree resin.

Master Mugwort nodded along to the monologue before making his exit.

Shortly thereafter, the King of Zhao fell from his horse and injured his ribcage. His doctor's prescription was: "We must apply one-thousand-year-old blood to the area."[28] And so a royal order was sent down to procure the blood, but none could be found.

Master Mugwort told the King, "Here at court there's an alchemist who is several thousand years old, no less! Let's kill him and take some of his blood; being even older it should take effect all the faster."

The King was overjoyed to hear this, and discreetly sent someone to seize the alchemist.

Facing his doom, the alchemist prostrated himself on the ground and wept, "My own parents only just turned fifty! The old lady living next door to the east brought us some wine to celebrate their longevity, and I drank until I was completely off my face. Before I knew it, I'd taken my exaggerations too far. To tell the truth, I haven't lived a thousand years! Venerable Sir Mugwort is most adept at telling tall tales. Pay him no heed, my King!"

The King of Zhao cursed at the alchemist, but let him go.

The rice sack's secret (FS:8)

The wife of Li Ji of Yan was beautiful yet wanton and engaged in an affair with a young man from the neighborhood. When Ji caught wind of this, he conspired to catch them at it. One morning, he hid himself away to spy on them. He saw the young man enter the house and bolt the door shut, at which point he stood up and knocked.

"It's my husband!" cried out the wife in shock. "What do we do?"

The young man looked at her and asked, "Is there a window somewhere?"

"There's no window," she said.

"How about second door?"

"There's no other way out."

"Then how am I going to escape?"

The wife's eyes landed on a cloth sack hanging beside the bed. "That could work."

So the young man clambered into the sack, crouched against the bed and said, "If he asks about it, just pretend I'm a sack of rice."

The wife unbolted the doors to let Ji in, and he searched all over the room for the man to no avail. Eventually he reached the side of the bed and noticed the lumpy sack that was too heavy to lift. "What's this thing?" he probed. The wife was terrified, and she stuttered and stammered away, unable to answer the question Ji kept shouting at her.

少年恐事露，不覺於囊中應曰：「吾乃米也。」季因撲殺之，
及其妻。艾子聞而笑曰：「昔石言于晉，今米言于燕乎？」

[FS:9]

齊有病忘者，行則忘止，臥則忘起。其妻患之，謂曰：「聞
艾子滑稽多知，能愈膏肓之疾，盍往師之？」其人曰：
「善。」於是乘馬挾弓矢而行。未一舍，內逼，下馬而便焉。
矢植于土，馬繫于樹。便訖，左顧而覩其矢曰：「危乎，流
矢奚自，幾乎中予！」右顧而覩其馬，喜曰：「雖受虛驚，
乃得一馬。」引轡將旋，忽自踐其所遺糞，頓足曰：「踏却
犬糞，污吾履矣。惜哉！」鞭馬反向歸路而行。須臾抵家，
徘徊門外曰：「此何人居？豈艾夫子所寓邪？」其妻適見之，

29 Translation from Durrant 2016, 1436–1437.

Inside the sack, the young man was petrified at the thought their affair would be exposed. Without thinking, he prompted her, "I'm rice, damnit!"

With that, Ji beat the young man to death, and then did the same to his wife.

When Master Mugwort heard of this, he laughed and said, "Long ago in Jin there was a stone that talked. And now it would appear that in Yan, there was a sack of rice that told of a similar story."

Here Master Mugwort references a record in *The Zuo Tradition* (*Zuozhuan* 左傳), in which an instance of a talking stone in Jin is relayed to court as an potential omen. The resulting discussion blames the ruler for diverting resources towards his own comfort rather than the people's welfare: "When a person is not timely in attending to his affairs, grudges and enmities stir among the people, and mute things speak."[29] What Mugwort is implying, then, is that had Li Ji attended more keenly to the needs of his wife in the first place, he would not have ended up being confronted by this sack of talking rice.

The forgetful man of Qi (FS:9)

In the State of Qi, there lived a man who was plagued by memory loss. When he was going somewhere, he would forget to stop when he got there, and when he lay down, he would forget to get back up again.

His wife was worried about him. "I hear that the humorist Master Mugwort knows many things. He'll be able to find a cure for even the most incurable of illnesses. Why not try to seek his advice?" she suggested.

"Good idea!" replied her husband.

So he set off by horseback, bow and arrow under his arm. But before he had even made it ten miles, he felt his insides clench. Dismounting his horse, he stuck his arrows in the ground, hitched the horse to a tree and took a dump.

After finishing his business, his eyes fell onto the arrows in the ground to his left. "How dangerous!" he cried, "Where did that stray arrow come from? It almost got me!" Then, glancing to his right he spied his steed, and delightedly declared, "Well, despite that false alarm, I seem to have found myself a new horse!" But when he took hold of the bridle to turn the horse around, he trod right into his own excrement. The man stamped his foot and bemoaned, "And now I've gone and stepped in dog shit. My shoe's filthy! What a mess!"[xxx]

He set back the way he had come, whipping his horse as he went. Before long, he had arrived back home. Loitering at the entrance, he muttered, "Whose house is this? How could this place be the abode of the great Master Mugwort?" At that point his wife caught sight of him,

知其又忘也，罵之。其人悵然曰：「娘子，素非相識，何故
出語傷人？」

[FS:10]

齊王好談相，士之以相進者，接踵於朝。有自稱神相者，介
艾子以見王曰：「臣鬼谷子之高足弟，而唐舉之受業師也。
卽臣之術可知矣。王亦聞之乎？」王笑曰：「寡人乃今日而
聞君矣。試視寡人何如？」答曰：「王勿亟也！臣相人必熟
視竟日而後言，言無不中。」於是拱立殿上以視。俄有使
者持檄入白，王色變。相者請其故。王曰：「秦圍卽墨三日
矣，當發援兵。」相者仰而言曰：「臣見大王天庭黑氣，必
主刀兵。」王不應。須臾有人著械入見。王色怒。相者問其
由。王曰：「此庫吏，

---

30 On physiognomic terminology and physiognomic practices in general, see Wang Xing
     2020.

31 The "Master of Ghost Valley" Guiguzi 鬼谷子, was a well-known Warring States thinker,
     with several writings on physiognomy attributed to him. Tang Ju was a Warring States
     physiognomist, probably male. Hence, the "promising disciple" remark places our phys-
     iognomist among ludicrously esteemed company.

and realizing that he must have forgotten where he was going yet again, she started to yell at him. Much chagrined, the man responded, "Lady, this is the first time we've laid eyes on one another! Why are you saying such hurtful things?"ˣˣˣⁱ

The Physiognomist Extraordinaire (FS:10)

Physiognomy (*xiangshu* 相術) refers to the practice of reading a person's fate and character based on their physical features, especially those of the face. Practitioners of physiognomy made a living by offering fortune-telling consultation services.[30]

The King of Qi had a penchant for consulting physiognomists. Accordingly, physiognomists far and wide fell over each other to be introduced by ministers at court. There was one self-styled "Physiognomist Extraordinaire" who obtained an audience with the King via Master Mugwort's introduction. Once at court, he declared, "Your servant was the most promising disciple of the Master of Ghost Valley, and the one that taught Tang Ju his trade.[31] From this my skills can be known! Has word of them preceded me, perchance?"

The King chuckled and said, "Today was the first We'd heard of your skills! But do have a go at reading Our face and see what you think."

To this the physiognomist replied, "Pray do not rush things, my King. When this humble servant of yours performs physiognomy, he must familiarize himself with the appearance of his subject for an entire day before submitting his verdict. That will ensure not a single word is off-mark." And so the physiognomist remained in the throne room, where he stood in a respectful bow observing the King.

Presently there entered a palace attendant carrying the draft of a formal call-to-arms to report to the throne. At this, the King's composure wavered. The physiognomist inquired as to the reason, and the King replied, "It has now been three days since the State of Qin laid siege to Jimo, so We shall have to send in the relief troops."[32]

The physiognomist peered up and said, "Your servant knew You would be confronted with military matters when he noticed the black energies of His Great King's Heavenly Court."[33] The King did not respond.

Soon thereafter, a man in shackles was brought to the throne room. Upon catching sight of him, the King's expression darkened. The physiognomist inquired as to the reason, and the King replied, "This store-

32 Jimo was a settlement in Qi territory. See map.
33 Central point of the forehead.

盜金帛三萬，是以囚之。」相者又仰而言曰：「臣見大王地角青色，必主失財。」王不悅曰：「此已驗之愍，請勿言。但言寡人終身休咎何如爾！」相者曰：「臣仔細看來，大王面部方正，不是箇布衣之士。」艾子趨而前曰：「妙哉，先生之相也！」齊王大笑。相者慚而退。

[FS:11]

虞任者，艾子之故人也。有女生二周，艾子為其子求聘。任曰：「賢嗣年幾何？」答曰：「四歲。」任艴然曰：「公欲配吾女子老翁邪？」艾子不諭其旨，曰：「何哉？」任曰：「賢嗣四歲，吾女二歲，是長一半年紀也。若吾女二十而嫁，賢嗣年四十；又不幸二十五而嫁，則賢嗣五十矣。非嫁一老翁邪？」

---

34 The chin area.
35 Wang Xing 2020, 103–108.

room attendant made off with thirty thousand in cash. He is here to be sentenced to imprisonment."

The physiognomist peered up once again and said, "Your servant knew You would see riches go astray when he noticed the turquoise hue of His Great King's Earthly Horn."[34]

The King was not amused. He said, "We ask that you tell Us no more of the tribulations We have already suffered and instead speak only of the fortunes and misfortunes We can expect to encounter in Our remaining days."

To this, the physiognomist replied, "Having studied my Great King's visage in minute detail, I have perceived the shape of His face to be square and upright, and do declare that he is not your average plebian!"

Master Mugwort rushed forth to intervene and cried, "Marvelous indeed, this gentleman's 'physiognomizing'!"

The King of Qi hooted with laughter and the humiliated physiognomist made his exit.

Physiognomic knowledge being esoteric and specialized in nature paved the way for fraudsters like the character described here, since the recipient usually had little way of knowing whether or not the reading was correct. There had long been a level of suspicion, especially among literati, surrounding the accuracy, morality, and performative elements of physiognomic practices.[35] In this case, not only was the performative element not convincing enough, but also left the underlying trick clear to all.

Master Mugwort proposes a marriage match (FS:11)

Yu Ren was an old friend of Master Mugwort. Yu had a daughter who was two years old, and Master Mugwort suggested he promise her to his son.[36]

Ren said, "How old is your worthy scion?"

Master Mugwort replied, "Four years old."

Ren flushed with anger and said, "You want me to marry my daughter to an old codger?!"

"What?" said Master Mugwort, confused.

Ren said, "Your worthy scion is four years old, my daughter is two. That's double her age! Say my daughter marries at twenty, your worthy scion would be forty. And if she is so unlucky as to marry at twenty-five, then your worthy scion would be fifty! How is that not marrying an old codger?"

---

36 Since people were considered one year old at birth, the daughter and son are slightly younger than this. The original numbers have been preserved for the sake of the punchline.

艾子知其愚而止。

[FS:12]

齊宣王謂淳于髡曰：「天地幾萬歲而翻覆？」髡對曰：「聞之
先師，天地以萬歲為元，十二萬歲為會。至會而翻覆矣。」
艾子聞其言大哭。宣王訝曰：「夫子何哭？」艾子收淚而對
曰：「臣為十一萬九千九百九十九年上百姓而哭。」王曰：
「何也？」艾子曰：「愁他那年上何處去躲這場災難？」

[FS:13]

艾子畜羊兩頭於囿。羊牡者好鬥，每遇生人則逐而觸之。

37 Kutcher 2018, 1–2; 27–42; Tsai 1996.

With that, Master Mugwort realized he was being silly and gave up on the plan altogether.

Here, just as in *Master Mugwort's grandson* (FS:6), Mugwort is given a taste of his own medicine, with Yu Ren feigning a complete lack of comprehension of the concept of time in order to gently dissuade his old friend from a proposal he is not prepared to accept.

King Xuan asks Chunyu Kun about the world (FS:12)

King Xuan of Qi asked Chunyu Kun, "After how many myriad years will the world start over?"

Chunyu Kun replied, "According to my late teacher, a period of ten thousand years is known as a 'cycle' and a period of one hundred and twenty thousand years is known as an 'epoch,' and when it reaches that point everything will start over."[xxxii]

Upon hearing this reply, Master Mugwort burst into loud sobs. Taken aback, King Xuan blurted, "Dear master, what are you bawling for?"

Master Mugwort bit back his tears. "I am crying for the people in the year one hundred and nineteen thousand nine hundred and ninety-nine."

"Whyever might that be?" asked the King.

"I feel so dreadfully sorry for them! When that year comes, how will they escape this terrible catastrophe?"

Mugwort's exaggerated reaction exposes his ruler's preoccupation with immaterial events in the distant future instead of the pressing issues of his time, along similar lines to the wall-building episode in MS:10. Another possibility is that this rests on a pun on the word *fanfu* 翻覆, which can mean to flip over, as in to reset and start from the beginning, but also to physically flip over. In other words, King Xuan is asking when the year count will reach the end of its cycle and start from the beginning, but Mugwort interprets the question literally: when will the world flip upside-down?

Master Mugwort's billy goat (FS:13)

A perennial presence in the ruler's residence throughout Chinese history has been eunuchs: the castrated palace attendants who could be entrusted with the necessary jobs inside the imperial complex without impregnating a member of the emperor's harem. Their proximity to the emperor and the resulting opportunity to get involved with politics often generated mistrust and derision among the scholar-official class.[37]

Master Mugwort kept two goats in a pen. The billy goat was fond of tussling, and every time he encountered a stranger he would chase and

門人輩往來，甚以為患。請於艾子曰：「夫子之羊牡而猛，請得閹之，則降其性而馴矣。」艾子笑曰：「爾不知今日無陽道的更猛裏。」

[FS:14]

艾子晨飯畢，逍遙於門。見其鄰擔其兩畜狗而西者。艾子呼而問之曰：「吾子以犬安之？」鄰人曰：「粥諸屠。」艾子曰：「是吠犬也，烏乎屠？」鄰人指犬而罵曰：「此畜生，昨夜盜賊橫行，畏顧飽食，噤不則一聲。今日門闢矣。不能擇人而吠，而群肆噬齧，傷及佳客，是以欲殺之。」艾子曰：「善。」

---

38 Matsueda (1970, 96) suggests that here it is used for slovenly army troops.
39 Wilkinson 2022, 39.16.

butt him, much to the dismay of Master Mugwort's disciples whenever they paid a visit. They petitioned Master Mugwort, saying "Dear master, that billy goat of yours is so violent! We implore you to get him fixed. That'll settle him down."

Master Mugwort laughed and said, "Haven't you heard? These days once the balls come off they get a lot more violent!"

Dogs to the slaughter (FS:14)

When Master Mugwort was relaxing by his gates after breakfast one day, he noticed his neighbor heading in a westerly direction with a dog in both baskets of his shoulder-pole.

"My good fellow, where are you going with those dogs?" shouted Master Mugwort.

"To sell them to the butcher," replied the neighbor.

"But they're guard dogs—why have them slaughtered?"

The neighbor pointed at the dogs and cursed them. "These blasted creatures! Last night a bunch of thieves went on the rampage in my house, and what did my dogs do? They watched on in fear with their full bellies, without letting out a single yelp. Then when morning arrived, they flew out through the open gates and ran amok, barking at people indiscriminately and biting willy-nilly, and an important guest of mine ended up getting hurt! And that's when I decided they must die."

"Sounds good to me!" said Master Mugwort.

The clue to this one lies in the neighbor's remark about the dogs' full bellies. It is a jab at members of society who receive a salary from the state, yet do not perform when push comes to shove (staying quiet during the robbery), while misdirecting or abusing their powers the rest of the time (the indiscriminate barking and biting). Calling someone a "dog" (quan 犬, gou 狗) was a generic insult, but as we have seen in Miscellaneous Stories, it was often used for officials and other members of the bureaucracy.[38]

The fortune-teller's bride (FS:15)

Both in premodern times and today, it has been common practice across East Asia to calculate a person's destiny from the year, day, month and hour of birth. This is done by finding the equivalent stem-branch value in the sexagenary cycle, which results in a set of eight characters. Each of these carries its own set of particular values, as well as associations with the Five Phases and the animals of the Chinese zodiac, which are used to make predictions about the fortunes and misfortunes the person can expect to encounter at different stages of their life.[39] The calculation could be a factor in important life decisions involving another person, such as entering into marriage, as we shall see in the following episode.

[FS:15]

艾子通五行，多與星士游。有南里先生者，其刎頸交也。娶妻而求全。每聞一女，必相其容德，推其命造，務底於善而後可。故久而不就。一旦為媒氏所誤，娶得醜女。曰頭深目，皮膚如漆，雖登徒之婦不至是也。南里先生不悅。艾子往賀之曰：「賢閣容色之妙，某聞之審矣。弟未知庚甲，願以見諭。當為吾子推之。」南里先生閉目搖手而答曰：「辛酉、戊辰、乙巳、癸丑。」艾子拊掌而退。

---

40 Marriages were often arranged without a prior meeting between the couple, sometimes with a professional or amateur matchmaker acting as a go-between between the two families.

Master Mugwort was conversant in the arts of astrological calculation and regularly consorted with fortune-tellers.[xxxiii] Among these was Master Nanli, and the two fellows were inseparable.

In choosing a wife, Master Nanli wanted the complete package, so whenever a match was in the works, he would make sure to have a physiognomy reading done to measure the girl's virtue and calculate her destiny from the timing of her birth. Only if everything down to the last boded well would Nanli assent to the match, and as a result he had been without success for a rather long time.

One day, he was misinformed by the matchmaker and ended up marrying an ugly girl with a head like a mortar, sunken eyes, and lacquer-like skin.[40] Not even the wife of Dengtu could hold a candle to this girl.[41] Master Nanli was not best pleased.

When Master Mugwort dropped by to offer his felicitations, he said, "The features of your esteemed bride are just as incredible as I'd heard. However, I am yet to learn her birth date characters. Do let this little brother of yours in on the secret, so he can re-do the calculations for you."

Master Nanli closed his eyes wearily and waved him off the idea. "They're *xinyou, wuchen, yisi, guichou*."

Master Mugwort clapped his hands in delight and took his leave.

Regardless of any positive fate they may spell, these eight characters sound much like "That new wife of mine is monstrously ugly."[42] It would seem Master Nanli's preoccupation with finding an auspiciously destined bride led him to overlook some other—perhaps more basic—bridal criteria.

41 In the "Rhapsody on the Extent of Master Dengtu's Lechery" 登徒子好色賦, the Warring States figure Song Yu 宋玉 describes the ugliness of Dengtu's wife in vivid detail. Dengtu appears in person in *Lordships and lovelies* (OS:22).

42 *Xinyou, wuchen, yisi, guichou* are most likely 新有屋陳已似鬼醜.

艾子外語

[OS:1]

齊宣王置酒雪宮，召艾子而樂焉。艾子故豪酒，飲大觚，嚼大臠。司觴者承王命進觚，誤投以醯。王起壽，艾子盡飲，蹙額俯伏辭曰：「臣醉不勝杯酌矣！」王曰：「先生豪酒，其誰不知！寡人為壽而託醉焉，無乃闕禮于執事耶？」艾子稽顙曰：「大王賜臣，臣折腹矣。」王顧左右，曰：「頃進者醯也。」宣王大笑，扶艾子起曰：「寡人之罪也。」洗醆更酌，一座盡歡。

[OS:2]

艾子少孤而竇，捉襟肘見，穿屨指露。景丑氏造焉。應門童子，身無寸縷，下體以瓦覆前後醜惡。景丑氏問曰：「顧邪？倩邪？」

1　The palace is the winter retreat of the Qi kings, in present-day Zibo 淄博, about 100km northeast of Ji'nan, Shandong.

2　While translated literally here, this phrase is a common expression indicating an impoverished lifestyle.

Outer Sayings of Master Mugwort

A banquet in the Snow Palace (OS:1)

King Xuan of Qi threw a banquet in the Snow Palace and summoned Master Mugwort to make merry with him.[1] Master Mugwort was, as ever, a prodigious consumer of wine; he devoured it by the gobletful along with large quantities of meat.

At the King's command, the wine-bearer brought forth the goblets, but he had accidentally filled them up with vinegar. The King raised a toast to longevity, and Master Mugwort downed his cup, wrinkled up his face, and threw himself forward onto the floor in apology: "Your servant has reached his limit! He cannot drink another drop!"

King Xuan said, "The Venerable Sir is unmatched in his talent for drinking—of this we are all well aware! Your lord has made a toast to longevity. If you excuse yourself on account of being already too drunk, would that not show a lack of etiquette on your part?"

Master Mugwort got onto his knees, pressed his forehead against the ground, and cried, "Have mercy upon me, my Great King! My belly has taken a hit!"

King Xuan glanced at his attendants, one of whom said, "What they presented him with just now was vinegar." The King boomed with laughter and helped Master Mugwort to his feet, saying "Our bad, Our bad." The cups were washed and refilled, and the rest of the banquet was thoroughly enjoyed.

Master Mugwort's childhood (OS:2)

When Master Mugwort was little, he was fatherless and impoverished. So tattered were his clothes that his toes peeked out from his slippers, and if one pulled on his lapels his elbows would have poked through his sleeves.[2] When Mr. Jingchou paid him a visit at home, he was greeted by a doorboy with nothing to cover his body but two tiles over his unsightlinesses at the front and the back.[3]

"Is he the hired help, or just doing you a favor?" asked Mr. Jingchou.[xxxiv]

---

3   A Mr. Jingchou appears in *Mencius* 2B.2, as a Qi grandee upon whom Mencius somewhat reluctantly relies for lodgings. See Eno 2016.

艾子曰:「非也,彼自饗飧,我與衣裳。」

[OS:3]

齊潛王為世子,艾子為傅。書十日而不成誦也;字五日而
不成畫也。艾子曰:「甚矣,世子之憒於學也!」以狀告宣
王。王曰:「先生謬矣!吾使人入宮覘世子,見其展書據几
而撫掌,似悟于書之趣也。」翌日,世子出閤,艾子問曰:
「昨者宮中展書,據几撫掌而樂,有諸?」世子曰:「然。」
「然則何樂?」答曰:「始知書籍是板鏤。」艾子遂行。

[OS:4]

艾子好飲酒,九吐而不減其量。聞淳于髡善酒,往造曰:
「先生名酒,千古絕倡,一斗亦醉,一石亦醉。

---

4   The translation of Chunyu Kun's dialogue in this episode amalgamates two existing *Re-
    cords of the Historian* translations by Wai-yee Li, and Giulia Baccini and Maddalena
    Barenghi, respectively. For the source text, see Li 2013, 110–111, and Nienhauser 1994–,
    vol. XI, 152–155; *Shiji* 126.3199.

"Neither," replied Master Mugwort. "He got the food today, so I got the clothes."

Master Mugwort tutors the crown prince (OS:3)

King Xuan of Qi was succeeded by his son, King Min, who would go down in history as a cruel and imperceptive monarch who heeded bad advice and put to death many a loyal advisor who dared attempt to rectify his ways. He ended up on the run and was finally cornered and executed by one of his ministers, explicitly citing the king's utter obliviousness towards state matters.

Back when King Min of Qi was the crown prince, Master Mugwort was his tutor. The prince would try to memorize a book for twenty whole days and still be unable to recite it, and he would practice writing a character for five days and still be unable to write it from memory.

"It is grave indeed, the heir's dimness in his studies!" cried Master Mugwort, before reporting the predicament to his father King Xuan.

"The Venerable Sir is mistaken!" responded the King, "I sent someone into the inner palace to spy upon the crown prince, and he was seen with a book laid out on the table, clapping his hands. It would seem that he has in fact been awakened to the joys of reading."

The next day, as the prince departed from the library, Master Mugwort asked him, "I am told that yesterday you were in the inner quarters with a book laid out on the table, clapping your hands in amusement. Was that the case?"

"It was," replied the prince.

"Then what was so amusing?"

"It was the first time I realized books are printed!"

So Master Mugwort went on his way.

Master Mugwort challenges Chunyu Kun to a drinking contest (OS:4)

The following episode transplants Chunyu Kun's famous remonstration of King Wei of Qi in the *Records of the Historian* Humorists chapter (see "The Humorists paradigm") into a conversation with Mugwort. The original speech was used to persuade King Wei to rein in his wine-fueled revelry; here it turns into a game of one-upmanship as to which man can hold his wine best.[4]

Master Mugwort was a heavyweight when it came to wine; at the point where most would have thrown up, he would just keep on drinking. Upon hearing that Chunyu Kun could likewise hold his alcohol, he paid him a visit and said, "Sir, your fame as a wine-drinker is unrivaled by any who has ever lived. You can get drunk with one dipper just as well

僕可勉斾。今居我右，願營壁壘，以終惠教。」

　　淳于髡問曰：「賜酒大王之前，執法在傍，御史在後，髡恐懼俯伏，可飲一斗。親有嚴客，髡帣韝鞠䠶，侍酒於前，奉觴上壽，數起而飲，可盡二斗。斯兩者，子能如我乎？」艾子曰：「不如。」淳于髡曰：「朋友交游，久不相過，卒然相覩，歡然道故，可飲六斗。州閭之會，男女襍沓，六博投壺，相引為曹，握手無罰，目眙不禁，可飲八斗而醉二參。日暮酒闌，合尊促席，男女同坐，履舄交錯，杯盤狼藉，堂上燭滅，主人留髡，羅襦襟解，惟聞薌澤。髡心最歡，可飲一石。斯三者子能如吾乎？」艾子曰：「不如。」淳于髡曰：「此皆不如，欲居我右，何呢？」

艾子曰：「醞釀羅漿，滿甕浮香，有酒且飲，無酒莫嘗。吸若奔濤，咽若漏囊。初夜再旦，跋扈飛揚。醒不涓滴，

5　The six rods and pitch pot are drinking games.

with a bushel. Abject as I am, I am prepared to push myself harder in this field. At present, your powers are greater than my own, so I have come in the hope that I may perch at your ramparts to benefit from the full extent of your teachings on the matter."

Chunyu Kun said, "If the occasion in question is that wine is being bestowed upon me in the presence of the King, with the Upholder of Precepts at my side, and the Attendant Scribe behind me, then bowing low and drinking in trepidation, I can drink one dipper. If the occasion in question is that my in-laws are treating an important guest, and I am bowing on my knees with rolled up sleeves and attending upon the guest who drinks first, toasting longevity, and standing up and down and up again, then I can drink two dippers. In these two situations, are you a match for me?"

"I am not," replied Master Mugwort.

Chunyu Kun said, "If the occasion in question is that I am catching up with a friend I've suddenly run into after a long while, and we are chatting merrily about the good old days and exchanging our innermost feelings, then I can drink six dippers. And if the occasion in question is a party in the districts or villages, when men and women mingle, playing the six rods and pitch pot, calling on each other to form couples, holding hands without censure and staring or flirting without prohibition, then I can drink eight dippers and remain only twenty percent drunk.[5] And when the sun sets and the wine runs low, when we pool the wine that is left and squeeze together with men and women sitting at the same table, with shoes mixed up and dishes in disarray, before the candles in the hall are snuffed out and the host asks me to stay the night, when the silken lapels are untied and I catch the first whiff of their perfumed skin—on occasions such as these, my heart is at its most ecstatic, and I can drink a full bushel. In these three situations, are you a match for me?"

"I am not," replied Master Mugwort.

"If you are no match for me in any of those situations," said Chunyu Kun, "then how do you propose to ever best me?"

Said Master Mugwort,

"O—
That fermented wonder we all know as wine
Its buoyant aroma so fragrant and fine:
In any proportion, you name your amount,
I'll ingest it all
Streaming into my mouth.
From the start of the night 'til the break of the day
My drunken performance

醉不骯髒，客盡離披，主鮮頹唐。千鐘百觚，差可比方，溫溫克克，無怠無荒。謔浪笑傲，曾不否臧。子能如我乎？」淳于髡撫然有間，曰：「是則髡之所以不如也。讓艾先生居右。」

[OS:5]

齊大夫餉主爵銀萬兩，拜銀青。望風者餉金萬兩，拜金紫。又有餉玉萬塊者，歲餘不報。走告艾子曰：「餉銀銀青，餉金金紫，餉玉寂寥。願先生私問之。」艾子以齊大夫之語語主爵。主爵曰：「玉皇大帝是孤闕，尚未得處。」艾子哈咳而退。告齊大夫曰：「惜公生較晚，不及覲取青紫如拾芥之世而謀諸。」

---

6   During the Han dynasty, the "Commandant of the Nobles" was an official title prefix that granted responsibility over the nobility in the capital. During the Sui and Tang, it referred to the "Bureau of Honors," a unit of the Ministry of Personnel, which was in charge of awarding noble titles (Hucker 1985, 180).

Sustains the part-ay.
I drink up when sober; permit me one boast
My stellar decorum!
The pride of my host.
Beaker or goblet, a hundred or more,
A thousand, a million!
The rest hit the floor.
The life of the party, the best in the land,
My joking and teasing
Not once out of hand.[xxxv]
So, would you say you're a match for me?"

Chunyu Kun pealed with laughter and said, "If that's what we're talking about, then I cannot claim to be your equal. Top spot is yours, Venerable Sir Mugwort!"

Gifts for the Commandant of the Nobles (OS:5)

A Qi grandee gifted the Commandant of the Nobles ten thousand ounces of silver, and was appointed to the silver-seal blue-ribbon rank of government.[6] An opportunist observer gifted the Commandant of the Nobles ten thousand ounces of gold, and was appointed to the gold-seal purple-ribbon rank of government.[7] Later, somebody gifted the Commandant ten thousand pieces of jade, but for more than a year there was no return on the bribe.

He sent word of the matter to Master Mugwort. "The guy who gave him silver got a silver-seal rank, and the guy who gave him gold got a gold-seal rank, then I gave him jade—and nothing! Venerable Sir, I do hope you might make a discreet inquiry as to what has happened."

Master Mugwort duly told the Commandant what the grandee had said, and he replied, "As of yet there are no open vacancies over at the Great Jade Emperor's, so I haven't been able to place him."[8] Master Mugwort snickered and took his leave.

When he reported back to the grandee, he remarked, "It's a pity you were born in this day and age and missed out on the hallowed era when 'seals and ribbons were as easy to pick up as weeds off the ground.'"

---

7   The official seal bequeathed by the state upon members of the official bureaucracy was evidence of position and rank. It was carried on one's person and often came with a ribbon-cord as decoration. "Silver seal with a blue ribbon-cord" and "golden seal with a purple ribbon-cord" corresponded to particular high-level ranks.

8   This emperor is the Daoist god-ruler of the Heavens. See also *The Jade Emperor's birthday party* (OS:11).

[OS:6]

東蒙山中人喧傳虎來。艾子采茗，從壁上觀。聞蛇告虎曰：「君出而人民辟易，禽獸奔駭，勢烜赫哉！余出而免人踐踏，已為厚幸。慾憑籍寵靈，光輝山岳，何道而可？」虎曰：「憑余驅以行可耳。」蛇於是憑虎行。未數里，蛇性不馴。虎被緊纏，負隅聳躍，蛇分二段。蛇怒曰：「憑得片時，害却一生，冤哉！」虎曰：「不如是，幾被纏殺！」艾子曰：「倚勢作威，榮施一時，終獲後災，戒之！」

[OS:7]

莒之大夫墨而盲于政；莒之小吏蕩而盲于目。吏屢愆期于畫諾也。久之，且來。大夫詰之，吏曰：「目眚。」大夫曰：「吾視汝目青青白白。」吏曰：「然，公視吏青青白白，吏視公糊糊塗塗。」艾子謂：「小吏之對也佞。」

9　Now known as the Meng 蒙 mountains, part of the Yimeng 沂蒙 mountain range in Weifang, Shandong province.

The joke here, of course, is how literally the Commandant interprets the bribes. Gold and silver were easily matched, but when faced with jade, which carried no obvious connotations of any particular rank or position, his best guess as to what the briber might be after was a role working for the Jade Emperor, the celestial ruler of Heaven and Earth.

The Snake and the Tiger (OS:6)

Up in the Dongmeng mountains, people were shouting to relay a warning that a tiger had been sighted.[9] Master Mugwort had been out gathering tea-leaves and looked on from the top of a precipice.

There, he heard a snake talking to the tiger: "When you show up, the humans back out of your way and the birds and beasts scatter in fear—what commendable majesty! As for me, I consider myself lucky if I can show up without getting trampled on. I would like to take advantage of your good favor and exude magnificence throughout the mountains! But how?"

Said the Tiger, "Hop aboard and you shall see."

So the Snake mounted the Tiger's shoulders. But before they had gone a mile or so, the Snake could not contain his natural urges any longer and the Tiger found himself uncomfortably constricted around the neck. Caught in a tight spot, he pounced, leaving the Snake cut in half.[10]

"I relied on you for one moment and ended up losing my life!" fumed the Snake. "The injustice of it!"

Said the Tiger, "Well if I hadn't, I would have nearly been strangled to death!"

Master Mugwort remarked, "If you take advantage of borrowed power to throw your weight around, you'll get your moment in the limelight, but it will only end in disaster. Be warned!"

The short-sighted magistrate of Ju (OS:7)

When it came to matters of governance, the magistrate of Ju was stupid and short-sighted, while his lazy clerk could barely see anything out of his actual eyes! The clerk would regularly miss his deadlines for signing off on documents. After this had gone on for a while, the magistrate questioned him about it, and the clerk said, "I have cataracts."[11]

"Your eyes look clear enough to me!" said the magistrate.

"Exactly," replied the clerk, "My eyes may look clear from your perspective, but when I look at you, Sir, all I see is a jumbled mess!"

Said Master Mugwort, "Not bad, the clerk's retort."[xxxvi]

---

10 Reference to *Mencius* 7B.23 on cornered tigers. See Eno 2016.
11 Opacity of the cornea, not necessarily a cataract by modern definitions.

[OS:8]

艾子在平陸，與其友道上行。有乘軒者來。其友誡艾子曰：「此吾至親也，避之。」有擁蓋者來。曰：「此吾至友也，避之。」行十數處，皆然。已而有弄蛇者來，有逐疫者來，艾子一如其友之誡誡其友。其友愀然曰：「胡子親友貧窶至此哉！」艾子曰：「富貴者汝盡攘去矣。」

[OS:9]

泰山東麓木偶曰惡來，神甚靈異。惟時淫潦縱橫，橋為之圮。人以木偶為梁而徒涉之。游閒公子過而憫曰：「豈有木偶神而為梁者乎？」拂拭安置，敬禮而去。惡來怒，將祟公子。比隣木偶讓曰：「不祟徒涉而祟敬禮，其理殊昧。」惡來曰：「既往難咎。見在不懲，吾忿何洩？」公子被祟，陳牲醴祈而獲寧。泰山西麓惡獸曰孤獨，如熊而人言，善咥人。

---

12 In roughly Warring States Lu. Present-day southwest Shanxi province, close to the Henan border.

Upmarket carriages (OS:8)

Master Mugwort was walking along the street in Pinglu with a friend.[12] There appeared a fine coach, and the friend alerted Master Mugwort, "Here comes a close friend of mine. Let's give way to him." There soon came along another fancy carriage with a draped awning, and he said, "I am on most excellent terms with the passenger in there, so let's give way to him." This was followed by several further such instances as the pair continued on their way.

After a while, a snake-charmer came by, and then a shaman-healer appeared. For both, Master Mugwort alerted his friend to give way to them, just as his friend had before.

His friend looked concerned. "How did these close friends of yours fall into such abject poverty?"

"Because you snapped up all the rich and noble ones!" retorted Master Mugwort.

At the foot of Mount Tai (OS:9)

At the eastern foot of Mount Tai was a wooden idol called Mavolāgatha, whose spirit was of unusual potency. One year during the rainy season, a flood swept through and wrecked the bridge. People started using the wooden idol as a bridge instead, stepping along it to cross the stream. A passing Loafabout Lordy took pity on the idol.[13] "A spirit-idol being used as a bridge? Surely we cannot have that!" He wiped the idol down, put it back in place, paid his respects and went off on his way.

Mavolāgatha was fuming and set about putting a curse on the Lordy.

"You didn't curse any of those guys who trampled on you," reproached the wooden idol next to him. "Yet here you are, cursing the one who paid his respects to your spirit! That doesn't seem fair."

"You could hardly condemn the other ones for doing as they did," rejoined Mavolāgatha. "But if I don't wreak retribution on this one now, how am I going to vent my resentment over it?"[xxxvii]

The Lordy was afflicted by an evil presence, and only after laying out a sacrifice of meat and wine and praying was he able to live in peace once more.[14]

Over at the western foot of Mount Tai there was a malevolent beast by the name of Loner, who looked like a bear but could speak like a human and was prone to devouring them.[xxxviii] Loner had been trapped in a

13 *Youxian gongzi*, the idle son of noble family with plenty of money and time on his hands. See Records of the Historian 129.3271.
14 Compare with *Bigger baddies* (MS:29).

虞者獵較，籠獨檻車，將糜焉。遇熱腹先生過之，獨於檻中乞哀曰：「我生不辰，大命將戕。公是熱腹，無得冷腸！拯我斧鑕，出我鑊湯。」先生聞語，大起悲涼。乘虞間暇，若已徬徨，爰啟鐍鑰，輒解轙靷。獨方出檻，爪牙大張。遽搏先生，將見殞亡。先生曰：「捄汝瀕危，而反咥我，為善者懼矣！」獨曰：「狼子野心，何厭之有。不知退避，以當吾前。釋汝而去，饑渴何賴。」竟咥熱腹先生。艾子曰：「游閒好義招祟，熱腹好仁遭咥，甚矣仁義難輕施也。籍令兩君若弗聞也者而過之，人議忍而不情；與之周旋，又議憨而多事，有好心，無好報，然哉！」

[OS:10]

艾子之友海翁善謔，林客嗜諧，三人為刎頸交，居九曲之塢。有夸毗子者，衣冠談笑，無弗似艾子者。行經塢曲，值兩翁逍遙于門，揖而語曰：「叟之遠來，得無有意惠教耶？」夸毗子曰：「余有謔癖，久病方甦，

15　A slight twist on "[Enough to] strike fear into the good/talented ones" (*wei shanzhe ju* 為善者懼), which refers to a predicament whereby a ruler is known to show favoritism, resulting in courtiers making suggestions that aim to please him, while proposals deemed less pleasant to his ears are held back to the detriment of the overall governance.

caged cart by a forest warden on the hunt, who was now getting ready to make mincemeat of him.

At that point, Mr. Sympathy-Guts happened to pass by. Loner begged him from between the bars, "Fate has come to smite me before my time is up! Dear sir, warm-hearted Sympathy-Guts, don't go cold on me now. Spare me the butcher's block and the fiery cauldron!"

His plea for mercy gave rise to a surge of pity in Mr. Sympathy-Guts, and he took advantage of the warden's absence to loiter closer, unlock the cage and undo the fetters and bindings. But as soon as he was out, Loner bared his teeth and claws and pounced. In mortal peril, Sympathy-Guts cried out, "I came to your aid in your hour of need and now you turn around and eat me? 'The do-gooders must live in terror!'"[15]

"The voracious appetite of a predator knows no satiation!" retorted Loner. "You should have known better and stayed well out of my way, yet here you are right in front of me. Anyway, if I let you run off now, how am I going to appease this grumbling stomach of mine?" And that was the end of Mr. Sympathy-Guts.

Master Mugwort said, "The Loafabout's penchant for righteousness got him cursed, while Sympathy-Guts' penchant for humaneness got him mauled to death. Indeed, humaneness and righteousness cannot be dished out lightly. Say the two gentlemen had continued on their way pretending not to hear, people would conclude they were unfeeling and apathetic. Then again, if they do a good turn, the verdict is that they are fools who should have minded their own business. What goes around does not always come around, forsooth!"[16]

The misadventures of Master Suck-Up (OS:10)

Master Mugwort had two friends known as the Sea Codger and the Forest Lodger. The Sea Codger was given to cracking jokes, while the Forest Lodger was taken with jibes. These three bosom buddies were living beside a dock on a meander of the Yellow River.

There was a certain Master Suck-Up, who both in costume and banter bore some resemblance to Master Mugwort. As he strolled along the winding embankment, he happened upon the two old men putting their feet up in front of the gates.

"Old fellow!" said Codger and Lodger, with their hands clasped in greeting. "You have come far—might you have some wisdom to impart upon us?"

Master Suck-Up replied, "Well, I was once afflicted by an addiction to jokes which plagued me for some time, but at long last I have recovered.

---

16 More literally, "one is not guaranteed a positive return on an act of kindness."

願承清燕以罄玄談。」兩翁以姓字請。夸毗不知為艾子密友
也,答曰:「艾子。」兩翁心笑之,而謬為恭敬,曰:「耳曳
之名舊矣。治病何若?」答曰:「余抱痾三載,服艾七年,
故得舌本不強,牙後生慧。」須臾,艾子至。敘禮訖,夸毗
未嘗識艾子也。問客何來。兩翁曰:「艾子。」夸毗愧而欲
遁。艾子曰:「無傷也。適余見獲鷯者,問之。曰:魚池苦
群鷯竊啄,乃束芻為人,被簑載笠,持竿植之池中以懼之。
初佪翔不即下。漸審下啄。久之,時飛止笠上,恬不為驚。
因竊去芻人,自披簑載笠而立。鷯乃下啄,飛止如故。人隨
手執其足。鷯奮翼假假。人曰:先故假假,今亦假假耶?一
笑而任其遁去。

17 Mugwort is a medicinal herb used for ingestion and moxibustion which doubles, of
    course, as the family name of our protagonist. The teeth are wordplay, meaning also
    "learned how to parrot what other people say."

And now I'd like to use my newfound leisure to indulge in some idle banter."

Codger and Lodger inquired as to his name, and Master Suck-Up—unaware that they were good friends of the man himself—lied: "I am Master Mugwort."

The pair snickered between themselves. Putting on a show of great deference and respect, they cried, "A name that has long been familiar to these ears! Pray tell, how did you cure that affliction of yours?"

He replied, "I had the malady for three years, then took mugwort for seven, and thanks to that, the root of my tongue lost its rigidity and my teeth grew some wisdom."[17]

Before long, Master Mugwort himself arrived on the scene. By the time the ritual greetings were done, Master Suck-Up remained none the wiser, and asked where this traveler had come from.

"That's Master Mugwort," revealed Codger and Lodger. Mortified, Master Suck-Up was all set to flee.

"No harm done," said Master Mugwort. "Just now, I saw someone who had caught a cormorant, and asked him about it. He told me he was being constantly pestered by the thieving beaks of the cormorants by the fishpond, so he bundled up some straw to make a scarecrow. He draped his rain-cape over it, put his straw hat on top and a bamboo staff in its arm, then positioned it in the pond to frighten them. At first, the birds circled high above and wouldn't descend any closer. But slowly, they began to test the waters. And after a while, they would even perch on the hat from time to time, totally unafraid. At that point, the man discreetly withdrew the scarecrow and stood in its stead wearing the hat and cape. When a cormorant swooped low to fish and tried to perch on the hat, the man reached out and grabbed the bird's leg. It flapped around furiously, shrieking and cawing. The man said, 'Caw, caw'—yes, you better believe you've been *cawt*. Last time it was a scarecrow, but this one doesn't feel much like straw now, does it!'"[18]

They laughed and Master Suck-Up was permitted to scurry back off again.

---

18 Cormorants are fish-eating birds that make a guttural and repetitive cawing sound, slightly deeper in pitch than a raven. The onomatopoeia used for this cry in the episode (rendered in modern Mandarin) is *jia jia* (假假), which means "Fake, fake!" To translate the end of the story more literally, then: "The cormorant flapped around furiously, crying '*Jia jia!*' and the man said, 'The last one certainly was, but how do you like this for a fake-fake?'"

[OS:11]

艾子一日夢游玉帝所。值玉帝誕辰，百神入賀。獨一人在三天門下，進退維谷。翊衛者曰：「帝有旨，勑戴進賢冠者入。」其人遂冠進賢冠，得入，列班行。百神次第朝賀訖。其人趨前。帝問何官。其人對曰：「魁星。」帝曰：「汝左手所執元寶何在？」魁星指頭上進賢冠，對曰：「買了這箇。」帝又曰：「汝右手所執大筆何在？」魁星又指頭上進賢冠對曰：「有了這箇，丟了那箇。」玉帝退朝，艾子亦覺，謂弟子曰：「孰謂進賢冠佳！卽如魁星，司文章筆札者，只戴了此物，便廢却筆札。」

The Jade Emperor's birthday party (OS:11)

The deity Kui Xing started out as the Daoist god of part of the Big Dipper, but later came to symbolize literary talent, specifically success in the civil service examinations. With this new role came a stylized set of symbolic imagery: Kui Xing depictions tend to present him standing upon a giant tortoise or upon a carp transforming into a dragon, with a writing brush poised in one hand and a scholar's cap or ingot in the other. Statues and images of Kui Xing were widespread in the Ming, displayed as they were in the households of examination hopefuls as objects of veneration and luck.

One day, Master Mugwort dream-roamed to the palace of the Jade Emperor. It was the Emperor's birthday and all manner of deities had turned out to offer their felicitations. Yet there was one who lingered on outside the Gates to the Three Heavens, seemingly caught in a dilemma over whether or not to go in. When the Standby Guard announced, "The Emperor has issued the order that those endowed with the scholar's hat may enter," the deity plonked his hat on his head, gained entry, and joined the line of well-wishers. After all the other deities had offered their congratulations one by one, he hastened before the Emperor, who inquired as to which official position he held.

"I am Kui Xing," replied the deity.

"Then where did the ingot that you hold in your left hand go?" asked the Emperor.

"I used it to buy this," replied Kui Xing, pointing at the hat on his head.

"And what about the big brush you hold in your right?"

Kui Xing pointed at the hat on his head again and replied, "Well, once you've got one of these, you can forget all about that!"

With that, the Jade Emperor retired from court and Master Mugwort woke up. He remarked to his disciples, "What's so great about the coveted scholar's hat? Even if you're Kui Xing, the god of literary prowess himself, once the hat goes on, the brush goes out the window."

The *jinxian guan* was the hat worn by an official when attending an audience with the emperor. As a mark of the official career, we can read this episode as a cynical remark on the institution of the civil examinations, which acted as gatekeeper to such positions.

Price tags and land grabs (OS:12)

This episode takes us to the court of King Hui of Liang, a notable ruler of the central state of Wei (a.k.a. Liang), who is especially famous for having lent his name to the first section of *Mencius*. At his court this time, instead of Mencius we find Master Mugwort, who seems to be in an interlocutory position between

[OS:12]

齊宣王好大苑囿，地逼薛，將築焉。薛君恐，告急于梁惠王。王使艾子往說齊王罷之。薛君德梁王而獻地，并以盍大夫陳戴氏之食邑，及其弟仲子之於陵焉。仲子謂兄曰：「說梁，非艾子不可，而從臾艾子往者，隴斷父也。」盍大夫使御者公無辱致書隴斷父曰：「盍大夫戴敢告下執事，薛為不道，罔敦世講，陡獻盍於陵之地于梁，橫肆侵陵。請如魯仲連先生聊城故事，緩頰於艾先生。」隴斷父悉索敝賦，然後許行。復書盍大夫曰：「執事使使儼然辱命，以苟且盛行關節之時，亦養士之常也，匪獨佞一人。大夫無惜小費，以隳大業。敢布腹心。」公無辱復命。

---

19 Chen 陳 here is an alternative way to write Tian 田, as we have seen for the Qi royal bloodline. Chen Dai and Zhongzi were related to King Xuan, who also appears here.

20 See Eno 2016; *Mencius* 3B.10.

Qi and Wei. But we do meet two other characters of Mencian fame: Chen Dai and his brother Chen Zhongzi.[19] Zhongzi was a renowned moral paragon in his day, although his particular brand of ascetic morality drew only colorfully worded scorn from Mencius.[20]

King Xuan of Qi had a fondness for large leisure grounds. His lands abutted the fief of Xue, and the King was making preparations to appropriate them for that purpose. Growing anxious, the Lord of Xue sent urgent word of the matter to King Hui of Liang.[21] King Hui sent in Master Mugwort, who successfully persuaded King Xuan out of the idea. In gratitude for King Hui's assistance, the Lord of Xue offered him a portion of his land, along with the portion of land enfeoffed to Chen Dai, the Grandee of Ge, and Wuling, the dwelling of his younger brother Zhongzi.[22]

"When it comes to persuading King Hui of Liang, nobody but Master Mugwort will do," opined Zhongzi to his older brother. "And the only one who'll be able to cajole Master Mugwort into helping is the Elder of the Mound."

The Grandee duly had his attendant Sir Shameless send a letter to the Elder of the Mound which read: "Chen Dai, the Grandee of Ge herewith presumes to inform your good self that the conduct of the Lord of Xue is improper. In utter contempt for generations of good faith between us, all of a sudden he has offered the lands of Ge and Wuling to the King of Liang. An abominable violation! I implore you to do as the Venerable Sir Lu Zhonglian did for Liaocheng and have a word on our behalf with Venerable Sir Mugwort."[23]

But the Elder of the Mound wanted to make the most out of the opportunity before assenting to the plan. He wrote back to the Grandee of Ge to say, "Do not let me disappoint your good self, and instead hurry me on my way with a 'packet,' as is commonplace in hiring a gentleman. Wretched as I may be, I am not alone in this. Surely the Grandee does not begrudge a little expenditure to ensure success in his grand endeavor? I have herewith ventured to share my humble introspections."

Sir Shameless passed on the message.

---

21 Xue was a fief in Qi territory. Possibly, then, this "Lord of Xue" is the Lord of Mengchang or his father Tian Ying 田嬰.

22 Warring States Qi, inland area to the southeast of today's Shandong province. Ge 盂 for Ge 蓋. Wuling is often pronounced Yuling.

23 When the Qi city of Liaocheng was under occupation by Yan forces, Lu Zhonglian (also Lu Lian 魯連) persuaded the Yan king to withdraw by the means of a letter. Afterwards, Lu declined all rewards given in gratitude for his service, instead quietly slipping away.

仲子曰：「吾居於陵，所豐者黃壤，所處者玄蚓，顧安得長物乎？」乃見艾子，為言薛君獻地之由，斷父索賦之故。艾子怒曰：「人頭畜鳴，胡敢爾爾！」

旦日見梁惠王曰：「聞薛君德大王而獻地乎？」惠王曰：「得獻地，而後苑囿盡游觀之美。」艾子曰：「薛彈丸之地，割以獻，不足以固吾圉也。又益以盍。盍、齊先生封陳戴氏之食邑。薛君以詐而獻地，大王以勢而受地。齊自桓公九合諸侯以來，世號強齊。天下之地方千里者九，齊得十一。梁之不敵于齊明矣。務游觀之美，以招兵甲，竊為大王不取也。臣嘗受命大王以說齊，齊王從之。若受齊命以說大王，王從之乎？」惠王曰：「倏受獻而忽還地，寡人恥之。」艾子曰：「臣固知大王恥之矣。一旦齊王興問罪之師，將何辭以對？夫勇莫大於機未形而還地，恥莫大于師已興而還地。齊王若并薛而取之，豈惟大王之辱，寔臣為說之愧矣。」惠王起謝曰：「寡人慮不及此。微先生幾為薛君所詐，貽笑隣國。」遂却獻地。

24 Some intertextual wordplay here with Mencius's earthworm analogy. See Eno 2016.
25 Duke Huan of Qi formed an alliance of several polities, through which Qi first rose to prominence back during the Spring and Autumn period.

Zhongzi said, "The only thing that is plentiful in my home of Wuling is yellow earth, and the only thing found there are those black earthworms![24] As if we have expendable goods to give him!" And with that he went to meet with Master Mugwort himself, to inform him of Lord of Xue's offer of land and the bribe-seeking incident with the Elder of the Mound.

"Cries of beasts from the heads of men!" fumed Master Mugwort. "How dare they do such things!"

The very next day, Master Mugwort had an audience with King Hui of Liang. He said, "I hear that the Lord of Xue has made an offer of land as an expression of gratitude to the Great King?"

King Hui replied, "Yes, We have received the lands as offered, and they will someday prove themselves a leisure ground of the utmost beauty."

"That miniscule sliver of Xue land he has sliced off as an offering could hardly be claimed to shore up our borders alone," replied Master Mugwort. "So he added on Ge as a bonus, which had been enfeoffed to Mr. Chen Dai. The Lord of Xue has offered this land on a fraudulent basis, and Your Majesty has accepted it just because you can! Now, ever since Duke Huan forged the alliance of the sundry marquises, Qi's strength has been its renown.[25] All Under Heaven contains but nine divisions of a thousand miles and Qi controls one of them.[xxxix] Liang is obviously no match for Qi. Inviting enemy armies in pursuit of a scenic pleasure ground is not a path I would take, were I, abject as I am, in Your Majesty's shoes. In the past, your servant accepted a mission to persuade Qi on Your Majesty's behalf, and the King of Qi complied. If now I persuade Your Majesty on the behalf of Qi, will you acquiesce?"

"But to accept the lands and then abruptly return them would be a great embarrassment for this unworthy King," admitted King Hui.

"Your servant is well aware that this would cause the Great King some embarrassment. Nevertheless, how do you plan to explain yourself when the King of Qi raises his armies for a punitive operation? Courage would come no greater than averting the crisis before it materializes by returning the lands. Meanwhile, no embarrassment could be greater than if the lands had to be returned under the threat of armed conflict. In the event that the King of Qi annexes Xue and takes it away, Your Majesty would not be the only one left embarrassed. Frankly, it would be a great shame of my own to have been your consult on the matter!"

"We did not realize this was the case," said King Hui.[xl] "Were it not for you, Venerable Sir, I would have fallen for the Lord of Xue's tricks and become the laughing-stock of all the neighboring states." He subsequently returned the land offering.

艾子亦絕隴斷父，署其門曰：「惟須墐戶塞門，莫再鼓舌搖唇。」

[OS:13]

魏信陵君飲于賣漿者薛公家，過食鱠殘，患河魚腹疾。詰朝，夷門監侯生，舉秦不二善醫，知人爪生髮長，筋轉脉搖。信陵君使中涓召之。秦不二詢信陵君所由致病。中涓告以故。秦不二入診左手曰：「表實裡虛，病得之食鱠殘多。」信陵君曰：「然。」復診右手曰：「胃强脾弱，病得之食薛公家鱠殘。」信陵君曰：「然。」艾子听然而笑。侯生曰：「何笑秦不二也？」

---

26 From the *Classic of Poetry,* "Bin feng."
27 For an overview, see Hsu, *Pulse Diagnosis in Early Chinese Medicine.*

Master Mugwort also cut ties with the Elder of the Mound, writing a message on his gates: "One only need 'plaster up the windows and stop up the doors.'[26] Don't go sowing discord with that wagging tongue of yours again!"[xli]

The riverfish's bowel curse (OS:13)

In premodern China, a pulse reading was the first point-of-call for doctors aiming to diagnose which of the organs in the body were responsible for an illness, and to this day, Traditional Chinese Medicine practitioners must master an elaborate schema of diagnostic pulse-reading theories and practices.[27] Inevitably, not all doctors had a firm grasp on these, as we shall discover in the following episode.

Wei's Lord of Xinling went to Master Xue the wine vendor's place for drinks, where he overindulged in noodlefish, and picked up 'the riverfish's bowel curse.'[28] The next day, Scholar Hou, watchman of the Yimen Gate, recommended Qin Bu'er, a talented physician who understood the growth of the nails and the hair, every twist of the energy channels and every turn of the blood vessels.[29] The Lord of Xinling sent one of his retainers to call Qin Bu'er over. The doctor inquired as to the reason for the Lord's ailment and the retainer duly informed him.

Qin Bu'er entered the Lord's room, checked the pulse in the Lord's left wrist and said, "The exterior flow is full of pathogenic energy, yet the interior is low on vital energy. This ailment was acquired through overindulgence in noodlefish."

"It was," said the Lord of Xinling.

Checking the pulse in his right wrist, Qin said, "The energy of the stomach is sufficient, yet that of the spleen is deficient. The ailment was acquired from the noodlefish at Master Xue's place."

"It was," said the Lord of Xinling.

Master Mugwort broke into a grin and let out a chuckle.

"What's so funny about Qin Bu'er?" asked Scholar Hou.

---

28 Wei Wuji, the Lord of Xinling, is the half-brother of King Anxi of Wei (see *King Anxi asks Master Mugwort about Qi* [MS:3]). Master Xue was a talented individual, who, unappreciated by men of influence, had gone into seclusion as a wine-vendor. The Lord of Xinling sought him out and took him on as a retainer. See Nienhauser 1994–, vol. VII, 393; *Records of the Historian* 77.2382–2383. The curse in question is diarrhea.

29 Hou Ying 侯嬴, a vassal sought out by the Lord of Xinling from a humble station, and another cameo from Wei Wuji's biography in the *Records of the Historian*. Nienhauser 1994–, vol. VII, 387–399; *Records of the Historian* 77.2377–2385.

艾子曰：「昔秦越人診脉而見垣一方人。今秦不二診脉而見江一方魚。醫不三世，不服其藥。秦氏奚止三世哉！」

[OS:14]

楚春申君持五戒。有牛齒衰，懸令曰：「牛老而瘠，不忍棄之。有能善養以盡天年者，予之嗇官。歲給芻粟。」下士第一人曰：「臣養之，調其饑飽，時其冷熱。天年既盡，火葬腹中，寢處其皮。」春申君曰：「犯殺戒。」不許。第二人曰：「臣養之如父母，饑飽冷熱，各以時施，天年既盡，敝帷埋之，不使烏鳶螻蟻，有所窺伺。」

30 Qin Yueren, nicknamed "Bian Que" 扁鵲 after the legendary physician to the Yellow Emperor, was a famous physician of the pre-unification period.
31 Berkowitz 2005, 174–178; *Records of the Historian* 105.2785ff.

"Well, in days past, Qin Yueren made his diagnoses by the pulse and could see through a wall to the person on the other side.[30] Then today, Qin Bu'er made a diagnosis by pulse and can see through the river to the fishes within. They say, 'Take not the medicine of a doctor less than the third generation in his trade.' But it appears that in the Qins' case, it would be prudent to wait a couple more!"

There are many stories of Qin Yueren's impressive diagnostic and healing abilities, with his pulse-reading skills receiving special attention. He acquired a supernatural X-ray vision, and could not only see through walls, as Mugwort mentions here, but also through a patient's skin to the internal structures within.[31] Mugwort's remark at the end plays on the literal meaning of Qin Bu'er's name, "Not yet two."

The Lord of Chunshen's elderly ox (OS:14)

An adept and loyal vassal of Chu who once secured the release of his king from a hostage situation in Qin, Huang Xie, the Lord of Chunshen, remained at the height of Chu politics for over two decades. The Five Precepts (*wujie* 五戒, "Five Abstentions") are a basic code of ethics to which Buddhist laypeople adhere. They can be roughly summarized as abstention from taking life, theft, sexual misconduct, speaking falsehoods and intoxication.[32]

Chu's Lord of Chunshen was upholding the Five Precepts. He had an ox that was getting old, so he issued an announcement: "My ox is old and gaunt, but I cannot bear to forsake it. Whoever is able to care for it so that it may live out his allotted years, shall be made Husbander and provided with a yearly allowance of grain."[xlii]

One of his retainers said, "If I took care of it, I would feed it in accordance with its hunger and fullness and attend upon its chills and warmth. And when its time comes, I will give it a roasty cremation and inter it within my belly, then lay its hide to rest as my bedding."

"That would violate the Precept against taking life," replied the Lord of Chunshen. He did not grant the ox to the man.[xliii]

A second person offered, "I would take care of it as I would my own parents. I would attend upon its every need—hunger, fullness, chills, and warmth. And when its time comes, I shall bury it wrapped in tattered bed-curtains and allow neither the crows and the hawks, nor the mole-crickets and ants to have their way with it."[33]

---

32 Judging by the content, this character is also adhering to the "Ten Goods" (*shishan* 十善), a further list of abstentions. This could even be part of the joke; see "Anachronisms."

33 Bed-curtains are associated with horse burials in the *Records of Ritual* (*Liji* 禮記).

春申君曰：「犯綺語戒。」不許。第三人曰：「臣養之如子女，饑飽冷熱，舐犢之煦，嫗之天年卽盡，敝蓋瘞之，不令樵采眃眠，有所動搖。」春申君曰：「實語真語，不犯兩舌戒。」許之，如令。艾子曰：「客對無異詞。公子獨許第三。安知客語真實耶？」春申君曰：「漸近人情。」艾子出曰：「孟嘗養士，不辨賢愚。春申養牛，妄分真偽。」

[OS:15]

漢村有田舍翁，家貲殷盛，鄙而吝。浪蕩生謀曰：「翁富甲里中，不交當世，非所以光門閭也。」田舍翁曰：「子多長者之游，盍圖之。」浪蕩曰：「諾。」入藥肆，語王醫曰：「有持贄來者，可詐為艾子，受之。與若中分。」

34　For this anecdote with an accompanying illustration from the 1800s, see Liu Cifu 1966, 400.
35　In present-day Henan province, northwest of Zhengzhou.
36　*Zhi* 贄, a customary gift presented to an elder or senior upon the first meeting.

"This violates the Precept against verbal embellishments!" replied the Lord of Chunshen. He did not grant the ox to the man.

A third person suggested, "I would take care of it as I would my sons and daughters, watching over its hunger, fullness, chills, and warmth with all the tender affection of a mother cow licking her calf. And when its time comes, I shall inter it wrapped in tattered cloth, and let neither those who gather firewood nor those who work the land disturb it in any way."

The Lord of Chunshen said, "Words of sincere intent, words of truth, which do not violate the Precept against verbal two-facedness whatsoever!"[xliv] The ox was granted to the man, along with the promised title and yearly allowance.

Master Mugwort said, "Your retainers didn't have anything different to say, yet you granted permission only to the third. How did you know that one was speaking the truth?"

"What he said seemed slightly more humane," replied the Lord of Chunshen.

Master Mugwort made his exit and remarked, "It is said that in taking on retainers, the Lord of Mengchang makes no distinction between the worthies and the dullards. And it would seem that in taking care of his oxen, Lord of Chunshen makes baseless distinctions between truth and lies!"

The reputation-conscious Lord of Mengchang was famous for accepting new members to swell the ranks of his retinue, sometimes to the point of a lack of selectiveness (see FS:3). Here, no matter how the three bidders present their proposals, in reality the ox can expect the same level of treatment, yet the Lord of Chunshen is either too trusting or conveniently ignores this fact. This episode was probably inspired by a similarly-themed one from the career of Tu Benjun.[34]

The Master himself (OS:15)

There was an old farmer in Hancun who had built up household wealth, yet was greedy and miserly.[35] A Wandering Wastrel hatched a con. "Old fellow, you may be the richest man around here, but you don't rub shoulders with men of influence," he remarked. "At this rate, there's no way you'll be able to cast lasting glory upon your household."

"Your good self has several acquaintances in high places," observed the farmer. "How about you sort me out?"

"No problem," said the Wandering Wastrel.

The Wandering Wastrel went into an apothecary and said to Doctor Wang, "Someone is going to approach you with a gift of goodwill.[36] If you pretend to be Master Mugwort and accept it, I'll go halves with you."

王醫頷之。明日,浪蕩告富翁曰:「得艾先生矣。是魁梧特達,非侯王卿相,不與交眤者。諺曰:『堂堂皇皇,艾而如張,青眼流盼,四座生光。』若定交,富貴相資之道也。」翁乃具衣冠,持白璧一雙,文綺四端,介浪蕩見焉。既交,訑訑自矜。東郭順子娶婦,傾城往賀。艾子、王醫、富翁,浪蕩咸會焉。富翁指王醫語艾子曰:「是艾先生也。與余厚善。君知之乎?」艾子笑應曰:「知之。」傍觀者曰:「富翁瞶瞶,此非艾先生乎!」富翁往讓浪蕩。浪蕩曰:「一雙白璧,四端文綺,就交結真艾先生!」

[OS:16]

巴陵道上提籠者,低聲倡曰:「賣糕!」

艾子問:「于何而疾,奄奄氣息?」

答:「枵腹負擔,餒不允斥。」

37 See *Zhuangzi*; Ziporyn 2020, 165.
38 In present-day Henan province.

Doctor Wang nodded in agreement.

The next day, the Wandering Wastrel told the rich old man, "I've gotten hold of the Venerable Sir Mugwort for you. That's one exceptionally big fish—unless you're a marquis or a prince or a minister or the chancellor there's no way to rub shoulders with the guy! As the saying goes:

Boldly go and cast your net,
Mugwort-woven, laid and set.
Feel the warmth of nepotism,
Come and play prestige roulette!^{xlv}

If you can secure a rapport with him, we can call it a man of wealth and a man of influence mutually benefitting each other!"

And so the old man donned his formal attire and—clutching two white jade disks and four lengths of patterned silk—was introduced by the Wandering Wastrel to "Master Mugwort." Having made his acquaintance, the old man was positively bursting with self-satisfaction.

Some time later, when Master Non-Resist of the Eastern Wall got married, the whole city turned out to offer their felicitations.[37] Master Mugwort, Doctor Wang, the rich old man and the Wandering Wastrel were all present for the occasion. Pointing at Doctor Wang, the rich old man said to Master Mugwort, "That is Venerable Sir Mugwort, with whom I am on profoundly excellent terms. Are you likewise acquainted with him, good sir?"

"Indeed I am," chuckled Master Mugwort.

An onlooker blurted out, "Rich old man, you must be blind! The Venerable Sir is standing right in front of your eyes!"

The rich old man stormed off to give Wandering Wastrel a piece of his mind, who merely retorted, "Well, for just a pair of white jade disks and four lengths of patterned silk, you got to meet Master Mugwort himself!"

Master Mugwort meets a hungry vendor (OS:16)

On the way to Baling Master Mugwort came across a roadside vendor carrying a basketful of wares.[38] "Cakes for sale…" he mumbled in a deathly feeble voice.

Asked Master Mugwort:

Rasping and gasping, moaning and groaning,
Pray name the affliction by which you are pained.

Replied the vendor:

From my belly a mumble, a rumble, a grumble—
It clamors with hunger! Alas, I am drained.

問：「籠中有糕，何不取食？」

答：「糕之溲矣，去去售直。」

艾子曰：「決性命之情以饕利，昧是非之實以售利，鄙哉，鄙哉！」

[OS:17]

魯有迂滑二叟，踞石而談。迂叟曰：「余有百金，以十之二與若，若趨承我乎？」滑叟曰：「物不均，不得趨承。」「然則，平分之？」曰：「物已均，不必趨承。」「然則，全與乎？」曰：「物全歸，不用趨承。」諮于艾子。艾子曰：「強人趨承，迂叟迂哉！三不趨承，滑叟滑也！與其迂也寧滑。」

[OS:18]

艾子遊趙絕粮。南宮子猶唁之曰：「子門張羅，子突無烟，而令從者病乎？吾為輔車，先生緩頰于平原君，可乎？」艾子曰：「諾。」明日，南宮子猶遍告域中曰：「艾先生天下士也，

---

39 Likely an allusion to *Zhuangzi*. See Ziporyn 2020, 78.
40 To be exhausted to the point of desperation. *Analects* 15.2.

Asked Master Mugwort:

Dear vendor, that basket—I cannot but ask it:
Why not just bite into your cakes made of rice?

Replied the vendor:

They've been overheating, no good now for eating,
Be gone on your way, sir—or else name your price![xlvi]

Master Mugwort said, "A greed for profit that defies the love of life itself![39] Muddling what is right and wrong for the sake of making a sale! Despicable, despicable!"

Two old geezers on a rock (OS:17)

In Lu there lived two old geezers called Ol' Pretentious and Ol' Wily. One day, the two men were sitting on a rock having some banter.

Said Ol' Pretentious to Ol' Wily, "I have a great big pile of money. Say I gave you one fifth of it—would you be my lapdog?"

"No," answered Ol' Wily. "Unless the goods are fair and even, you wouldn't get me to be your lapdog."

"Then what if we went halves?" offered Ol' Pretentious.

"Well, if we had the same amount," replied Ol' Wily, "then I wouldn't have to be your lapdog."

"Then what if I gave it all to you?" said Ol' Pretentious.

"Well, if the whole lot was mine," replied Ol' Wily, "then there'd be no point in me being your lapdog."

When Master Mugwort was consulted on this matter, he said, "Forcing someone else to be your lapdog—Ol' Pretentious lives up to his name! And talking his way out of being the lapdog over and over again—so does Ol' Wily! But I'd take 'wily' over 'pretentious' any day."

Master Mugwort runs out of provisions in Zhao (OS:18)

Master Mugwort was traveling through Zhao and ran out of provisions.[xlvii] Nangong Ziyou expressed his condolences and made a suggestion: "Out alone in foreign lands, your hearth has ceased to make smoke. Have 'your followers fallen ill,' then?[40] Let's help each other out. I'll take the Venerable Sir under my wing if he has words with the Lord of Pingyuan on my behalf. How about that?"

"Agreed," said Master Mugwort.

The next day, Nangong Ziyou spread word throughout the whole area, saying, "The Venerable Sir Mugwort is a first-rate man of service. He affords

辨而有智，理枉能直，導滯必通，來為平原君重客。盍祈諸。」有殺傷人死者，挾白鏹求武。艾子至平原君門，曰：「狂且重辟，罪在不赦。」迴車而卻其鏹。有宦久不調者，餉青蚨求通。艾子至平原君門，曰：「彼墨狼藉，議在褫識。」迴車而返其蚨。有許人陰私者，餽珠璧求達。艾子至平原君門，曰：「大傷天理，必召奇禍。」迴車而復其璧。

南宮子猶不悅曰：「吾事先生，亦云勤矣。胡屢及平原君門而迴車乎？」艾子曰：「吾見平原君矣。始未言，而溫雅之容可掬；纔啟齒，而翹厲之色甚倨。是以口嚅嚅，足蹜蹜。故迴車。」南宮子猶曰：「欺余哉！」艾子曰：「有人在坐，何敢行欺！」問為誰。答曰：「藺相如。」南宮子猶曰：「藺相如前代聞人也。君豈說夢耶？」艾子曰：「原是說夢。」

41 The calamities are natural disasters and omens occurring in response to these immoral goings-on.

42 Nienhauser 1994–, vol. VII, 477–482; *Records of the Historian* 81.2439–2444.

OUTER SAYINGS OF MASTER MUGWORT

wisdom through disputations, straightening out the corrupt and guiding the bewildered to clarity.^{xlviii} He is soon to be the esteemed guest of the Lord of Pingyuan. Why not make a request of him?"

There was a man who had violently murdered someone, and he came carrying silver and requested that he be exonerated. But when Master Mugwort arrived at the Lord of Pingyuan's residence, he said, "He is guilty of a violent crime so grave that he must not be spared." So he turned his carriage around and declined the silver.

There was an official who had not been promoted in a long time, and he gave some cash and requested that a promotion be approved. But when Master Mugwort arrived at the Lord of Pingyuan's residence, he said, "That man is notoriously corrupt. The rightful thing to do would be to strip him of any position at all." So he turned his carriage around and returned the cash.

There was a man who had promised others their clandestine desires, and he presented pearls and jade disks and requested those desires be fulfilled. But when Master Mugwort arrived at the Lord of Pingyuan's residence, he said, "This would be a great violation of the Heavenly Principles and will invite extraordinary calamities."[41] So he turned his carriage around and gave back the disks.

Nangong Ziyou was displeased. He said, "I came to your aid and have kept to my side of the bargain assiduously. Why, then, do you keep turning your carriage around each time you visit the Lord of Pingyuan?"

Master Mugwort said, "I had the audiences with the Lord of Pingyuan. Before I spoke, he was all mildness and dignity. But as soon as I opened my mouth to make the request, his expression turned harsh and haughty! That look of his left my mouth a-stutter and my feet a-shuffle, and in my hesitation I turned my carriage around."

"Such deceit!" cried Nangong Ziyou.

"But with that man present, how would I dare be deceitful?" said Master Mugwort.

Nangong Ziyou asked to whom he was referring, and Master Mugwort replied, "Lin Xiangru."

"The famous Lin Xiangru of the previous generation? Are you sleep-talking or something?"

"Well, you've been daydreaming from the start," retorted Master Mugwort.

Lin Xiangru was a Zhao courtier and general. Mugwort's reluctance to conduct deceit before his eyes stems from a similarly themed story immortalized by the *Records of the Historian*.[42] At the time, Zhao was in the possession of a famous treasure known as "Mr. He's Jade" (*Heshibi* 和氏璧). In a sham ploy,

[OS:19]

齊客方方白者，平原君下士，亦曰陪堂，先意承旨，備出醜
態。有前知五世事者曰龜靈先生，談事有左驗，所至騷動。
趙王敬之如神明。送至平原君第。平原君奉以上座薰沐，
再拜稽首，而後問五世之事。龜靈先生曰：「公子一世為儀
狄，善釀酒。」平原君曰：「勝之酖酒有自來矣。」陪堂曰：
「旨哉，酒！臣想曾陪。」先生曰：「公子二世為伊尹，善
割烹。」平原君曰：「勝之食肉，職此之由。」陪堂曰：「雋
哉肉，臣想曾預。」

43 Yidi was a brewer in the time of Yu the Great, sometimes credited with the invention
of alcohol itself. Some sources, such as *Intrigues*, portray her as female, others as male.
(S)he was banned from making wine by Yu the Great, who was concerned about the
strength of her concoctions.

the King of Qin offered Zhao fifteen walled cities in return for the jade disk. Lin Xiangru was sent to Qin with the jade disk, and in a high-stakes stand-off at court, Lin shamed the Qin king for his deceit, lack of respect, and frivolous attitude towards state relations. In the end, Lin had the disk safely smuggled back over the border to Zhao.

The five lives of Pingyuan (OS:19)

Fang Fangbai, a guest-retainer from Qi, was a member of the Lord of Pingyuan's retinue. He was nicknamed "The Companion," sensing His Lordship's wishes and fulfilling them without instruction. He was good at guessing what others wanted to hear and fawning on them accordingly, often to the point of utter shamelessness.[xlix]

There was a clairvoyant by the name of Master Turtle Spirit who could perceive other people's past five reincarnations. The past-life experiences of which he spoke could be proven, and his arrival in Zhao had aroused a great deal of excitement. The King of Zhao viewed his supernatural insight with great reverence, and sent him over to the Lord of Pingyuan's estate as a gift.[l] The Lord of Pingyuan awarded Turtle Spirit the seat of honor and made sure to bathe and scent himself as a gesture of respect. Finally, after performing the ritual kowtows as an expression of the utmost reverence, he inquired as to the matter of the five lives.

"My Lordship," replied Master Turtle Spirit, "In one life you were Yidi, who had a talent for brewing wine."[43]

"So that is where my liking of wine comes from!" said the Lord of Pingyuan.

The Companion said, "I also find wine delicious! I guess I must have been in your company back then too."

The Master said, "In the second life you were Yi Yin, whose talents lay in the culinary arts."[44]

The Lord of Pingyuan said, "I see now that this is why I'm a meat-eater."[45]

The Companion said, "I find meat delectable, too! I must have been involved with you back then as well!"

---

44 Yi Yin was chief minister to Tang of Shang. In *Mencius*, this figure is frequently presented as a paragon of virtue, but in 5A.7, Mencius firmly dispels the rumor that Yi Yin came to Tang's attention through his cooking skills. See Eno 2016.

45 "Meat-eater" was a codeword for a high official or someone who had been granted a fief, such as the Lord of Pingyuan. See *Master Mugwort's next-door neighbors* (MS:32).

先生曰：「公子三世為膠鬲，隱魚鹽，周武王舉之，定鼎洛中。」平原君曰：「勝之嗜鹽，豈緣是耶？」陪堂曰：「臣亦自疑。」先生曰：「公子四世為屈原，秉忠貞。楚懷王逐之，行吟澤畔。」平原君曰：「勝之嗜水，或因此歟。」陪堂曰：「臣亦自疑。」先生曰：「公子五世為彭祖，周柱史，享年八百。」平原君曰：「勝壽幾何？」先生曰：「長可望一千，短可躋四百。」陪堂曰：「臣亦自喜。」

龜靈既出，平原君讓方方白曰：「先生所談，皆余五世事，於汝何預！越俎多言！」方方白免冠頓首曰：「臣備員陪堂，不如是無以獲歡于公子。既蒙誨論，敢不退避。」艾子曰：「世好奇而譚鬼，非獨平原與龜靈也。始為人欺，既而欺人，久之自欺矣。弟子記之，慎毋自欺哉！」

[OS:20]

毛空者，道聽塗說之輩也。艾子自楚反齊，毛空過焉。艾子詢新聞。

---

46 Jiao Ge was a peddler of salt and fish who was recommended as a worthy official to the final tyrant ruler of Shang, King Zhòu. In *Mencius* 6B.15, his background is mentioned in a passage about how the character of many a worthy man is wrought in a background of bitterness and hardship, with the fish and salt being one example. The implication, then, is not that Jiao Ge enjoyed this period of his life. See Eno 2016; *Mencius* 6B.15.

The Master said, "In the third life you were Jiao Ge, who hid himself away peddling fish and salt, before King Wu of Zhou recommended him to establish his new capital by the river Luo."[46]

The Lord of Pingyuan said, "Perhaps that's where my liking of salty food came from."

"I like it too!" said the Companion.

The Master said, "In the fourth life you were Qu Yuan. King Huai of Chu exiled him and he walked along the riverbanks chanting his verse."[47]

The Lord of Pingyuan said, "Perhaps my liking of river scenery is due to that."

"I like it too!" said the Companion.

The Master said, "In the fifth life you were Ancestor Peng, Censor of Zhou, who lived to the ripe old age of eight hundred."[48]

The Lord of Pingyuan said, "Then how long will I live?"

The Master said, "At the most we're looking at a thousand years, at the very least four hundred."

The Companion said, "I'm overjoyed as well!"

As soon as Turtle Spirit had left, the Lord of Pingyuan had stern words with Fang Fangbai. "The Master was here to tell me about my past five lives, which has nothing to do with you! Shut up and stay in your lane!"

Fang Fangbai took off his hat and descended into a kowtow. "I am at your service in the capacity of your Companion. If I can't fulfill that role, I have no other way to please Your Lordship. Having now received your censure, I cannot presume to remain in my position and hereby resign!"

Master Mugwort said, "His Lordship and Turtle Spirit are not alone in this world in loving the extraordinary and aggrandizing the supernatural.[li] At first one is deceived by others, then one deceives others, until eventually one deceives oneself. Disciples, take note! Beware of deceiving yourselves!"

Counting your ducklings (OS:20)

Hairy Airy was the type to indulge in roadside gossip.[49] When Master Mugwort arrived back in Qi from Chu, he bumped into Airy and inquired as to the latest news.

---

47 Qu Yuan was a poet and politician who composed many of the *Verses of Chu*. This was no pleasant stroll: having been spurned by his monarch, Qu famously drowned himself in a river.

48 Peng is a legendary figure famous for living an extremely long life. See *Master Mugwort meets an old woman in mourning* (MS:31).

49 The name is an allusion to the weightlessness of this character's unsubstantiated gossip. Alternatively, "Featherweight."

毛空曰：「人家一鳧產百子。」艾子曰：「無此理。」空曰：
「便是兩鳧。」艾子曰：「亦無是理。」空曰：「便是三鳧。」
漸至十鳧。艾子曰：「何不減子？」空曰：「吾寧加鳧，不
肯減子。」艾子笑而唯唯。毛空曰：「前月天雨肉一片，長
三十丈，濶十丈。」艾子曰：「無是理。」毛空曰：「便是
二十丈。」艾子曰：「亦無是理。」空曰：「便是十丈。」艾
子曰：「汝看世間，那得一片方圓十丈大肉乎？」問鳧產誰
家，肉雨何地。空曰：「行路人如此說。」艾子笑謂弟子曰：
「慎毋道聽塗說哉！」

[OS:21]

周太宰瀛璿介而察，繭絲細務，必親之。幾旬賵跪，

"One family had a duck that mothered one hundred little ducklings," replied Airy.

"That's impossible," said Master Mugwort.

"Then it was two of their ducks," said Airy.

"That's impossible as well," said Master Mugwort.

"Then it was three of their ducks," said Airy.

Airy continued in this vein until there were ten mother ducks.

"Why didn't you just lower the amount of ducklings?" asked Master Mugwort.

"I'd rather have more ducks than fewer ducklings."

Master Mugwort nodded and laughed.

"And last month a chunk of meat fell from the sky like rain," said Hairy Airy. "It was three hundred feet wide and a hundred feet thick."

"That's impossible," said Master Mugwort.

"Then it was two hundred feet wide," said Airy.

"That's impossible as well," said Master Mugwort.

"Then it was one hundred feet wide," came the reply.

Master Mugwort said, "Tell me, where in this world can one get hold of a giant piece of meat one hundred feet wide?" He proceeded to asked to whom the duck had belonged and where exactly the meat had landed.

"I heard it from someone I met on the road," responded Hairy Airy.

Master Mugwort laughed and instructed his disciples: "Take care not to 'repeat on the street what one has heard on the road!'"

This episode draws upon a remark by Confucius in *Analects* 17.14: "To repeat on the street what one has heard on the road is to abandon one's virtue," is an exhortation to verify one's sources before passing on potential misinformation like we see Hairy Airy do here, with Mugwort (somewhat hypocritically) placing himself on the receiving end.

Poetic justice for the Prime Minister of Zhou (OS:21)

The penultimate episode introduces a character embroiled in one of the vices of officialdom: spending so much time and attention on the minutia of day-to-day bureaucratic tasks as to render one oblivious to the bigger picture concerning the welfare of the populace. Here again, Master Mugwort is enlisted by others to assist, and presents this fastidious figure with a mock verse that is modeled around a court-case setup which bizarrely puts the fabled King Wu on trial for removing Zhòu, the final tyrant king of the Shang dynasty.

The Prime Minister of Zhou, Ying Xuan, was punctilious and fastidious. No matter how trifling a matter was, he would personally fuss over the minute details. There was unrest around the capital, so the sundry

庶僚大聚而謀，謂艾子善計，相率拜于其庭，祈焉。艾子曰：「諸君且休舍，徐圖之。」乃設詞曰：

「控訴處士伯夷叔齊，孤竹君二子，向緣伐商，叩諫天王，恥食周粟，隱于首陽，采薇采苦，築圍築牆。有暴男子曰管曰康，如熊如熊（羆），率虎率狼，毀我儲胥，侵我基疆，驚我婦子，伐我榆桑。兩造具備，宰允惟詳。鉏折豪右，驅剪強梁。靖安土著，雪慰遐荒。誰其證之，姜太公望。」

期日，太宰視篆。見詞，大索不得。歎曰：「胡為來哉！為法之弊矣！」輒以其務，歸于有司。

officials gathered together to decide what to do. One of them said he had
heard that Master Mugwort had a talent for fixing up plans, so they went
en masse to bow in his courtyard and beg his assistance.

"For now, go home and rest, gentlemen," said Master Mugwort, "I shall
come up with something in my own time." Presently he composed a ditty,
which went:

The Hermit Plaintiffs enter the courtroom. Boyi and Shuqi, sons of
Guzhu, state your grievance!

We accuse the "Heavenly" King Wu along with his henchmen,
     Guan and Kang!
He made the command
To his snarling band
To snatch our homeland.
A dynasty grand
So cruelly harangued.
And now left unmanned!
They face no remand.
Its return we demand!

The Accused stands present at court! What say you to these grave
charges?

Our King took the lead
And acted with speed,
Shang's citizens freed,
In their hour of need.
Thus all are agreed,
That our righteous deed
Was Heaven-decreed.
Not Guilty, we plead.

The testimonies of the two sides are complete. They are hereby related for judicious deliberation by the Prime Minister himself!"[lii]

One day, according to schedule, the Prime Minister was poring over
paperwork. He saw the ditty, but after racking his brains, he simply could
not figure out what it meant. "Who put this thing here?" he grumbled.
"It is a stain upon the office of the law." He got up and set aside his duties, delegating everything to an underling, and paid a visit to Master

及會艾子，曰：「先生周知民隱，來訪造詞。」艾子曰：「民隱難諮，太宰所謂自詒伊慼者乎！」留飲少間，太宰便去。弟子曰：「客去不留，禮歟？」艾子曰：「為其累坐也。觸政曰：不可與飲者歡場之劣焉。酒鑒曰：好做身分，主恭客傲，筋不沾唇，儼若木雕之人也。早去為幸。」

50 Quote from the *Classic of Poetry*. The original context has been interpreted to be about playing one's part in office while one still has the chance.
51 *Leizuo* 累坐 is drinking game jargon, but the remark simultaneously means "Because he's been implicated in the court case," or "He'd implicate me in the court case."

Mugwort. He said, "Venerable Sir, you know about the people's suffering. I have come to ask you about the wording of a ditty on this topic."

Master Mugwort said, "You've been making it hard for yourself to notice the people's suffering. The Prime Minister's predicament is a prime example of 'bringing grief upon oneself.'"[50] Master Mugwort invited the Prime Minister to drink, but he left after only a short while.

A disciple inquired, "You did not ask your guest to stay on as he was about to depart, Master. Was that proper etiquette?"

Master Mugwort said, "He'd have me forfeit![51] As the *Rules of the Goblet* state, 'One must not tarnish the blissful drinking arena with negativity.' And the *Mirror of Wine* says:

> As guest and as host, there are roles we must play:
> One must indulge while the other gives way.
> The banquet table's a sacred place,
> But for wooden statues there just ain't the space![liii]

That guy was just such a case: the way he sat straight-backed without even touching his chopsticks—the cheek! The sooner he's gone, the better.'"

Both texts quoted by Mugwort here are drinking game manuals, incongruously applied to a drinking situation outside of their remit. By luring the Prime Minister to his gates to ask about the poem, Mugwort has brought him out into the world to notice the unrest himself.

Lordships and lovelies (OS:22)

"Fish-from-Before," "Bitten-Peach," and "Jade-Luster," the names of the three male lovers in the following episode, are synonymous with the stories they invoke. "Fish-from-Before," for example, refers to an episode from the *Intrigues* in which the Lord of Longyang was out fishing with his lover King Anxi. After a string of successful catches, the Lord suddenly burst into tears, saying that he had been overjoyed with his first catch, but now having caught a few bigger ones, he found himself tempted to throw it back. Thinking of all the other beauties that might cross paths with the king, the Lord feared a similar fate for himself in the future: "Your servant weeps, for he was the fish You caught, Sire." The concern with eventual loss of favor that runs through these stories, together with the underlying expectation that male lovers were spurned or replaced as their youthful beauty faded with age, is key to this episode.[52]

---

52 For the original story, see Crump 1996, 417–418; Liu Xiang 1978, 917–918. For more on
    these particular textual tropes and representations of male homosexuality in pre-modern
    Chinese literature in general, see Hinsch 1990.

[OS:22]

前魚、餘桃、壁瑩者，魯孟孫、季孫、叔孫氏諸公子之少
艾，皆以變而嫛，服美驕矜，姕媚自喜。雖衛靈公之於彌
子瑕，楚靈王之於龍陽安陵，不是過也。南州大夫孺伯吊
廉成君喪，魚服而往，假道于薛。遇諸公子，挾少艾，沉
湎夜游，嗔隸嚆呵侮之，侵于大夫。魯平公聞而怒，將繫
惡少焉。諸公子懼，因登徒子季，託墻東先生，言于平公。
公曰：「以登徒之幸舍不備，寡人是耻，南州之皂隸受侮，
寡人是問。承教，其遣三艾為登徒紀綱之僕。」登徒辭公
曰：「臣無賴，少有陰陽之患。寔虛尊賜，敢歸璧于將命
者。」艾子以艾年問將命。將命屈指曰：「十五年前，齒方
十六。」

---

53 These three powerful clans, otherwise known as the "Three Huans" were descended
from Duke Huan of Lu. Possibly, Tu Benjun is indicating the original set of brothers.

Fish-from-Before, Bitten-Peach, and Jade-Luster were the young lovelies of Mengsun, Jisun and Shusun, noble scions of the State of Lu.[53] All three lads were gorgeous and thus the favorite of their respective scion. Self-satisfied and haughty in their fancy garb, comely and vain, the treatment they enjoyed even surpassed that shown by Duke Ling of Wey towards Mi Zixia, or by King Ling of Chu towards Longyang and Anling.[54]

When the Grandee of Nanzhou, Ru Bo, was grieving the death of the Lord of Liancheng, he put on a disguise and went on an incognito journey. En route via Xue, he ran into the trio of noble scions on a drunken night-time jaunt with their lovelies in tow. They flew into a rage at his runner and hurled threatening insults at him, before assaulting the Grandee.[liv]

When Duke Ping of Lu heard of this he was outraged and ordered the young ruffians bound up and arrested. The noble scions were terrified, so through Master Dengtu Ji they had Master East-of-the-City-Wall speak to Duke Ping on their behalf.[55]

The Duke said, "Your unworthy ruler was discomfited to learn of the staffing shortage at Dengtu's retainer lodgings, and inquired into the matter of Nanzhou being gravely disrespected as a lowly runner. We will take your advice and send the three lovelies over to Dengtu to be enlisted into his serving quarters."[56]

But Dengtu declined the Duke's offer, saying "Your servant has failed you! An inner conflict weighs upon my heart, and the gift you have bestowed is wasted on me. I must send these 'jade disks' home with the messenger."[57]

Master Mugwort inquired as to the age of the lovelies, and the messenger counted on his fingers before responding, "Fifteen years ago . . . they had just turned fifteen."

---

54   The story goes that Mi took a bite of a particularly delicious peach, and gave the rest of it to the Duke to enjoy. While at the time the Duke took this as affectionate, the relationship soured, and the Duke eventually reinterpreted the gift of a half-eaten peach as an insult. This episode's "Bitten-Peach" character is named for this. See Hinch 1990, 20–21; Yang and Li 1982, 118–119. Usually the Lords of Longyang and Anling are associated with two separate rulers. There may be some missing text here, or perhaps the two characters for "Longyang" were mistakenly inserted.

55   Master East-of-the-City-Wall is a byword for a hermit who has entered seclusion by taking up a commonfolk trade.

56   Reading between the lines, Dengtu (on whose lustful reputation, see FS:15) has told Master East-of-the-City-Wall to inform the Duke that he would like the three lovelies for himself, in a bid to allow them to escape a harsher sentence.

57   To return an item to its original owner. References the Mr. He's Jade story, on which see OS:18.

艾子撫掌曰：「諺云：男愛不弊軒，女愛不弊席。周書曰：
美女破舌，美男破老。則三艾者，須投之四裔，以禦魑魅
乎？」三艾向艾子泣曰：「吾儕小人，業已受屈，非復故吾，
乞緩牙後雌黃，冀諸公子猶可弄臾乎？」艾子許之。南州大
夫聞之，一笑而解。

58 The *Zuo Tradition* uses this precise wording to describe good-for-nothing or malignant
    royal relatives being dealt with in this way during the time of sage ruler Shun. See Durrant
    2016, 574–575. Mugwort might just be using this flowery allusion to indicate conscription
    to a far-flung garrison.

Pealing with laughter, Master Mugwort said, "As the saying goes, 'When a man is beloved, he does not wear out his carriage, and when a woman is beloved, she does not wear out her own sleeping mat.'[lv] And to quote the *Book of Zhou*, 'Fine women can bring ruin to the consort, and fine young men can bring ruin to the elders.'[lvi] As for these three lads, then, isn't it time they be thrown out into the wilds of the borderlands to help defend against demonic forces?"[58]

The three lovelies looked at Master Mugwort and wept, saying, "We lowly men have already suffered enough and repent our former actions. Help us erase our wisdom teeth, so that the noble scions can continue to enjoy their bedroom pleasures![lvii]

Master Mugwort assented, and upon hearing about the matter, the Grandee of Nanzhou laughed and let them go.

Appendix 1: Issues of Attribution in *Miscellaneous Stories*

The attribution of *Miscellaneous Stories* to Su Shi is not a settled matter, and the doubts over authorship date back to the Southern Song: "Word is that it was written by East Slope, but it is not certain that this is the case."[1] Regardless, by the Ming, which witnessed something of a *Master Mugwort* renaissance in terms of published editions and sequels, the association with Su Shi went virtually unchallenged.[2] Several editions carry his name as part of the title, while the work was included in published collections of his work such as Zhao Kaimei's *Five Assorted Works by East Slope*. Those against Su Shi's authorship view the association as a pre-existing spurious connection that was perpetuated by a culture of falsely attributed works in the fast-paced and market-propelled environment of the late-Ming publishing world. Qing bibliophiles subsequently tasked themselves with rectifying the consequences of this culture.[3]

In modern scholarship, the case for Su Shi's authorship was made by two articles in the late 1980s by Kong Fanli 孔凡礼 (1923–2010) and Zhu Jinghua 朱靖华 (1928–2008) respectively, both major figures in the study of Su Shi.[4] Taken together, these papers draw a variety of links between records that mention Su Shi having composed works on specific subject matter, and trace the personal connections of a Song poet who wrote about *Master Mugwort* directly to Su Shi himself. Of course, such approaches cannot supply conclusive proof, and at most only give greater credence to the possibility that Su Shi was the originator of at least parts of the received text. Approaches in the two articles and in recent work have involved drawing links between the *Miscellaneous Stories* subject matter and Su Shi's life, for example connecting the many waterborne journeys and sealife-themed episodes with Su Shi's time in Hainan, or pointing to stylistic or thematic similarities with works conventionally accepted as his. With a writer as versatile and prolific as Su Shi, that could perhaps be called low-hanging fruit, and such arguments conveniently ignore the fact that interests such as "ghosts and spirits" were likewise

---

1　Chen Zhensun 陳振孫 (1179–1262). Quoted in Kong Fanli 1985, 39.
2　With one known exception. See Section II, "*Master Mugwort* in the Ming."
3　On this phenomenon, see He Yuming 2013.
4　Kong Fanli 1985; Zhu 1989.

shared with many other writers of his day.[5] Both lines of argument are further undermined by Su Shi's celebrity status in his own time and in subsequent dynasties, which may have encouraged the composition of works that deliberately imitated his style and themes.

More recently, the issue has been revisited by Ahn Hei Jin 安熙珍, who, compelled by the nagging sense that *Miscellaneous Stories* did not have the feel of a Su Shi work, set about comparing the stylistic and thematic traits and vocabulary in *Miscellaneous Stories* with those found in established writings, concluding that: "We can be certain enough that Su Shi's compositional style is utterly dissimilar to the style of *Master Mugwort* and that the vocabulary that characterizes the content of *Master Mugwort* was not often employed by Su Shi. Based on the above inquiries into a variety of aspects, I do not believe *Master Mugwort* was necessarily composed by Su Shi."[6] Thus, recent attempts to prove and refute authorship share a dependency on which facets and texts have been selected from what is an amply documented life and a vast body of work to build the canon that has come to characterize him. This pick-and-mix approach can just as plausibly yield either verdict.

The authorship debate is just as much a story of the winding ways in which Su's vast body of surviving writings have been perceived, assigned internal levels of significance, and characterized down the ages, and of how the shifting landscape of social norms in readers' worlds in the meantime, especially with regard to the perceived acceptability of certain kinds of writing, have been invoked to opposite conclusions. This provides us with an opportunity to reflect upon our own assumptions and prejudices. Why is it that many have come to see a text of this nature, humor-filled and occasionally bawdy as it is, to be so especially incompatible with a figure of such literary greatness? Certainly, this marks a divide between ourselves and Ming readers, for whom the connection was clearly plausible.[7] And after all, of those more magnificent and serious writings that nobody thinks to question, how many enjoy a more directly traceable link to the hand of the man himself?

In sum, the only safe conclusion permitted by the available evidence is that we cannot know for sure either way. We may never know, and at present any movement in either direction seems unlikely unless fresh textual evidence or new digital methods come to light. What is more

5   Zhou Jin 2017, 9.
6   Ahn 2016, 139.
7   In this case, it seems that the Ming publishers involved did indeed believe the attribution. On Su Shi, humor, misonymy, and celebrity in Ming publishing, see "Wanli Humour Compilations and the 'Dongpo Vogue'" in Smithrosser 2021.

important in approaching these translations than Su Shi's actual level of input is the strong association with him these texts carried for their premodern readers. This is especially true for the Ming collections, which seem to have been composed in the firm belief that they were writing a sequel to a work by Su Shi himself. Doubt over the attribution is one of the reasons this text has not been more frequently read and thoroughly studied in modern times. But regardless of the author's identity, there is the simple fact that this is a work that was clearly widely read and regularly discussed down the ages. It is therefore deserving of our attention; to dismiss it today on account of a dubious authorial pedigree is to distort the shape of the Chinese literary tradition.

《五子諧策》序

五子諧策第十九。《艾子》三卷。宋蘇長公撰者，曰《雜語》。
明陸灼撰者，曰《後語》。屠本畯撰者，曰《外語》。《權子》
一卷，明耿楚侗撰。《憨子》一卷，亦本畯戲筆。都稱雜俎
云。明外史氏曰：《史記》載滑稽者七家，淳于髡、優旃、
優孟、王先生、東方朔、郭舍人、司馬相如。談言微中，廓
人主之禍心，譏當時之弊政，紀民情之險鄙。可笑，可談，
可警，可戒。非今之戲笑者所可彷彿也。其干齊楚趙魏之
君，似結靷憑軾之士。其機智似七家。其鑄詞似《短長策》。
由是讀者疑其有為而託之於寓言也。艾子不見傳記。海虞陳
眉公謂艾子事齊宣王。其書所載多後世之事。則艾子者或疑
實有是人

---

8   Tu's *Five Masters* refers to the individual collections of texts, as opposed to Master characters.
9   Courtesy name of Geng Dingxiang 耿定向 (1524–1596).

Appendix 2: Preface to *The Jest Intrigues of the Five Masters*

Number Nineteen, *Jest Intrigues of the Five Masters*.[8] There are three *Master Mugwort* fascicles: one by Gentleman Su the Elder of the Song called *Miscellaneous Sayings*; one by Lu Zhuo of the Ming called *Further Sayings*; and one by Tu Benjun called *Outer Sayings. Master Quan*, in one fascicle, is by Geng Chudong.[9] *Master Simple*, in one fascicle, is also of Benjun's playful brush. All of them are of the miscellany category. This Ming unofficial historian says: *Records of the Historian* biographized seven Humorist maestros: Chunyu Kun, Entertainer Zhan, Entertainer Meng, Venerable Sir Wang, Dongfang Shuo, Guo the Member of the Suite, and Sima Xiangru.[10] With "words of banter that indirectly strike a chord," they broaden the narrow minds of rulers, mock the faulty governance of the times, and document the perils and roughness within public sentiment.[11] As they laugh and banter, they caution and admonish. This is not something that the playful jokesters of today can reproduce. Master Mugwort stages interventions in the affairs of the Lords of Qi, Chu, Zhao and Wei in a way that is comparable to those traveling men of service.[12] His sharp-wittedness compares with that of the seven maestros, and his polished diction compares with that in the *Intrigues of Persuasion*.[13] As a result, its readers have suspected that it has been used deliberately to lodge messages.[14] Master Mugwort does not appear in the written record. As related by Chen Meigong of Haiyu, while Master Mugwort is in the service of King Xuan of Qi, his book contains many events from later ages.[15] Thus, some doubt that he actually existed and opine that it

10 The transmitted version of *Records of the Historian* does not include Sima Xiangru (c.179–117 B.C.E.). In early times we sometimes even see the figure of Sima Xiangru being used as a foil for the comic figures, as noted in Baccini 2011b, 163–164.

11 The quote is Sima Qian's encapsulation of the Humorists paradigm.

12 Probably indicates the "Four Lords," collected together in *Records of the Historian*: Mengchang, Chunshen, Pingyuan and Xinling, respectively.

13 Alternative name for the *Intrigues*. See Smithrosser 2021 for its significance in the Ming publishing world, and see Smithrosser 2022.

14 That is, as a fable (*yuyan* 寓言). The wording here mirrors that of Lu Cai (see Preface to *Further Sayings*), so it could be that Tu Benjun is pointing us towards Lu's speculations over Su Shi's intentions.

15 Chen Meigong is Chen Jiru 陳繼儒 (1558–1639).

或因蘇氏書而論之耶。姑置之矣。《權子》、《憨子》雖稍異《艾子》而託意實同。揔之，博諭醜類，滑稽之應諧使人自暢於天，鈞也。五子聯絡袞為諧策，以資賓戲。

長至日人倫堂書。

is a book by Mr. Su. For now, let us shelve the matter. Although *Master Quan* and *Master Simple* differ slightly from *Master Mugwort,* in the sense that meaning has been inserted into them they are in fact the same. In short, they broadly analogize the ugly things in this world, while the Humorist's jesting responses enable others to realize the will of Heaven of their own accord. In this aspect, they are equal, and I have brought these five *Masters* together to create a "Jest Intrigues."

> On the day of the Summer Solstice, Studio of Human
> Relationships[lviii]

Appendix 3: Table of Premodern Titles

The base editions used for this translation do not provide titles for the individual episodes. The titles are my own, chosen with an eye toward user-friendliness. However, some premodern editors of the first two collections *Miscellaneous Stories* and *Further Sayings* opted to affix titles to the individual episodes. These are displayed and translated below.

EPISODE #	PRECEDENT TITLE	TRANSLATION OF PRECEDENT TITLE
Miscellaneous Stories of Master Mugwort		
MS:1	*Shang zi* 傷子	Sad about his son
MS:2	*San wu* 三物	Three creatures
MS:3	*Leng zhai* 冷債	Unpaid debts
MS:4	*Xian muxu* 獻苜蓿	An offer of alfafa
MS:5	*Hao yin* 好飲	A fondness for drinking
MS:6	*Er ao* 二媼	Two old women
MS:7	*Zuan huo* 鑽火	Lighting a fire
MS:8	*Zhoushi* 舟師	The ferryman
MS:9	*Gan tu* 趕兔	Chasing rabbits
MS:14	*Fugui* 富貴	Riches
MS:15	*Wei liao gongshi* 未了公事	Unfinished business
MS:17	*Hao jienan* 好詰難	A fondness for questions
MS:20	*Song Fojing* 誦佛經	Reciting a Buddhist sutra
MS:21	*Mulü* 木履	The wooden clogs

MS:23	*Kedou* 蝌蚪	Tadpole
MS:26	*Yu zi* 愚子	Stupid sons
MS:27	*Maomao gui* 毛毛鬼	Hairy monster
MS:32	*Rou zhi* 肉智	Wisdom from meat
MS:34	*Hao wei shi* 好為詩	A fondness for composing poetry
MS:37	*Mai mao* 賣帽	Selling hats
MS:39	*Yanluo wang* 閻羅王	King Yama

Further Sayings of Master Mugwort

FS:1	*Wang fa* 王法	The way of kings
FS:2	*Suyuan* 訴冤	Airing grievances
FS:3	*Shike* 食客	Retainers
FS:4	*Jiang dao* 講道	Lecturing on the Way
FS:5	*Ren zhen* 認真	Recognizing the truth / Earnestness
FS:6	*Sun er* 孫兒	The son and the grandson
FS:7	*Dayan* 大言	Big words
FS:8	*Mi yan* 米言	The rice speaks
FS:9	*Bingwang* 病忘	Memory loss
FS:10	*Shen xiang* 神相	The amazing physiognomist
FS:11	*Lao pei* 老配	An old pairing
FS:12	*Yu ku* 預哭	Crying in advance
FS:13	*Muyang* 牡羊	The male goat
FS:14	*Shiquan* 噬犬	Guard dogs
FS:15	*Chou nü* 醜女	The ugly woman

List of Abbreviations

MS   Miscellaneous Stories of Master Mugwort (*Aizi zashuo*)
FS   Further Sayings of Master Mugwort (*Aizi houyu*)
OS   Outer Sayings of Master Mugwort (*Aizi waiyu*)

Text-critical Endnotes

i. The *jiumou* 蟹蛑 (also *youmou*), *pangxie* 螃蟹 and Peng Yue 彭越 are kinds of crab. According to the Song encyclopedia *Shiwu jiyuan* 事物紀原, the name of this crab was rumored to come from the early Han general Peng Yue, whose flesh-mince was delivered to regional lords as a delicacy (and probably also as a warning) after his execution. One revolted lord threw it into the river, where it turned into a crab. Matsueda suggests that the joke is the tininess of the Peng Yue crab compared to the stature of the figure who was its namesake (1970, 51–52). As for *yidai buru yidai*, there is an intertextual parallel with the description of a seafood banquet in the Northern Song text *Garden of Discussions by State Elders* (*Guolao tanyuan* 國老談苑), which ends with roughly the same punchline (Yimen Junyu 2013, 184). Mugwort's "a crab never lives up to the previous crab" spin went on to have a life of its own, but *Miscellaneous Stories* is the first documented appearance and may be the original source. Crabs also bear an association with the civil service examinations.

ii. This follows Yang Jialuo, Chen Weili and others in reading *yu* 竽 as *fu* 莩.

iii. Some editions give *chu* 怵, rather than the *xiu* 休 in the Gu edition on which this translation is based. *Chu* is arguably less redundant in the overall sentence and has been translated thus.

iv. This story, from the humour compilation *Grove of Laughs* (*Xiaolin* 笑林) (Matsueda 1970, 53), has been taken by some pre-modern commentators as a negative demonstration of the idea that blame or criticism should take into account the circumstances of the person at whom it was levelled, so as to be deserved and reasonable (責人當以其方也). The *Grove of Laughs* attributes this comment to Kong Rong 孔融 (153–208). See Chen and Guo 1996, 2.

v. The lackadaisical attempt of this magistrate (which for the purposes of this scenario we could imagine as akin to a mayor), who "shouted" (hu 呼) presumably because he himself is in the process of abandoning the city, is unlikely to be of any comfort to the elders of Ju, who, too infirm to flee, remain in the city to face their doom. A cynical remark on leadership. Another possible interpretation of this line is "Do not flee for now," as an attempt to retain manpower in the city to stay and fight.

vi. Reading *bi* 嬖 as *bi* 蹩. See Pinshiwen 2019.

vii. *Churu* 出入 "going in and out," seems to refer to a kind of disputative technique. Or, "You're lucky I wasn't busy with something!"

viii. Full quote as relevant to the passage: "When Yao possessed All Under Heaven, he did not hanker after the riches of his myriad subjects... He personally implemented frugal conduct in order to show his subjects the humaneness of looking after one another, so that they might live in harmony. Thus, he lived with untrimmed thatching for a roof and unsanded oak for rafters, his carriage unadorned and his woven mat unhemmed... and when he [abdicated and] passed down the entire world to Shun, he did so as easily as stepping backwards out of his slippers" (Liu An 1990, 404–405). The examples of frugality described in MS:14 are a combination of those listed in this *Huainanzi* passage with those listed in another (Liu An 1990, 320–321).

ix. Another possible interpretation of this line is "owing to this, he entered into an audience with [Xu] You [at his home]." What remains of the episode uses Xu You's full name to refer to him, rather than just "You" as here, and other versions of the rejection story depict Yao visiting Xu You. This would of course reverse the setting of the scenario, but the punchline works either way.

x. Compare this with a third *Huainanzi* passage: "Yao did not view possession of All Under Heaven as a prize, and thus conferred it upon Shun . . ." (Liu An 1990, 323–324).

xi. This episode places a twist on Xu You's rejection of the offer according to the transmitted version of events, which in fact sealed Xu You's image as a high-minded recluse immune to—or even repulsed by—the lures of power and reputation. One version of Xu You's response to the offer is related in the *Zhuangzi*: "The tailorbird lives in the depths of a vast forest but uses no more than a single branch to make its nest. When the beaver drinks from the river, it takes only enough to fill its belly. Go home, my lord! I have no use for an empire." Translation from Ziporyn 2009, 6. In case he had not made his determination clear enough, Xu You then fled and went into hiding, twice. It is the sheer vehemency of his rejection that makes him memorable amongst the many other figures who declined thrones throughout early Chinese history and legend, and also happens to afford extra punch to this particular punchline. Such a momentous proposal was surely seen to have called for a grand banquet. This adds another layer of humor to the minimalist setup.

xii. Reading *huo* 火 as *huo* 伙, as suggested by other editions which use *huo* 夥. Matsueda (1970, 53) translates this more elaborately as *kajiba-dorobō* 火事場泥棒, that is, a looter or someone who takes advantage of chaos for his own gain.

xiii. Reading *dizi* 弟子 as Aizi 艾子. If *dizi* is retained, the speaker here instead becomes one of Gongsun Long's disciples. Perhaps we should read this episode as a reversal of the Humorists paradigm, which sees the king exaggerating the laughable methods of the courtier to show him the error of his ways, or, at least, that he is wise to his tricks. It has been suggested that there was a performative aspect to the conceptual acrobatics for which Gongsun Long is famous, which may have been intended to amuse a ruler, rather than intended entirely seriously, despite many premodern commentators taking them as earnest sophistry (Harbsmeier 1998, 301).

xiv. See also MS:16, satirizing slightly different traits; MS:17 is more directly comparable with MS:13 on Qin Guli and the Lame Old Lady.

xv. Unlike his decisive father who had been hardened on the battlefield, Zhao Kuo was a theory-bashing sand-tables general who did not take the realities of war into account in his strategies. Despite several warnings, the King of Zhao sent him in anyway. According to *Records of the Historian*, at the time, the Zhao official Lin Xiangru made a similar analogy, comparing the decision to place Zhao Kuo in charge of the defense efforts to "gluing the tuning bridges to strum a zither" which, needless to say, was not the correct way to tune a zither (Nienhauser 1994–, vol. VII, 489; *Records of the Historian* 81.2446). Bai Qi immediately seized his moment to attack as soon as he heard that this inept general had been swapped in on the opposing side, thus the link between the installation of Zhao Kuo and the defeat at Changping was very direct indeed. The decision was also a result of the king ascribing a Qin agent's proposal greater weight than the repeated pleas from his loyal ministers and even from Zhao's own mother (and wife of his capable father). But here it is the lack of perceptiveness that is foregrounded: the fact that the king was unable, or refused, to see that Zhao Kuo was simply not up to a task of such gravity. This was obvious to everyone else, in a similar way to how the duck points out his evident physical unsuitability for catching rabbits in Mugwort's story.

xvi. This description is not quite what we see in *Records of the Historian* and *Intrigues*, according to which Zheng Anping first surrendered to the State of Zhao along with twenty thousand Qin soldiers, then two years later Wang Ji was found to be holding illicit discussions with other lords. I have kept the verb vague here.

xvii. Or "being categorized along similar lines to court entertainers."

xviii. Another possibility is to take *xu* as "to wait," which would render this line something like: "Then what are you waiting for, good sir? Let's give them a test—you ask one of them where the rice they eat comes from."

xix. A less likely possibility is that this refers to the ability to fulfill the princess's sexual needs. *Bu jie* 不潔 can also refer to having a strong libido. Another is the idea of obsequiousness, along the same lines as the metaphor of "brown-nosing" in English. There are many tales about Dragon Kings' daughters across Chinese folklore and literature. For some of those in English, see *Dragon Tales* 1988.

xx. More literally: "Newsflash, Bullhead Section Head: / The authority lies with King Yama, and not with you! / By all means to reduce the amount of official firewood / But you went too far by perverting the law for some leopard-skin loincloths."

xxi. The original is less specific: "Master Mugwort enjoyed composing poetry."

xxii. Many types of finals have faded out of Mandarin over time, which has resulted in some characters sounding deceptively close to each other, and potential rhymes between others being obscured. According to reconstructed medieval Chinese, both "hand" and the measure word for poems are *syuwX*. "Poem" is *syi* while "shit" is *syijX*. See Kroll 2017. What Mugwort hears from the room next door is "One poem" (*yi shou ye* 一首也), "And another poem" (*you yi shou ye* 又一首也), *shou* 首 being the measure word for poems. But his neighbor is in fact talking about his hand (*shou* 手): probably "I'll just use my hand" (*yi shou ye* 以手也)," and "I'll just use my hand again" (*you yi shou ye* 又以手也). There may also be a connection between the word "poem" (*shi* 詩) and "shit" (*shi* 屎), which in modern Mandarin, at least, would render "one poem" (*yi shou shi* 一首詩) and "a handful of shit" (*yi shou shi* 一手屎) roughly homophonic.

xxiii. Matsueda translates *saoya* more specifically as pertaining to *Lisao* from *Verses of Chu* and the *Daya* 大雅 section of the *Classic of Poetry*, while I have opted for the more general sense.

xxiv. Another possibility is to take *ya* 亞 as a mistake for *meng* 冡, which would render the passage: "The underlings simply could not think of a way around it, and confessed thus to the First Minister. He dwelt upon the matter at length before finally exclaiming, "Pfft, what about this one couldn't the Second Minister solve by himself?"

xxv. This line includes a missing *shi* 時, as suggested by Yang Jialuo 1967, ch. 4, 7. Pagination internal to chapter.

xxvi. It is possible that this passage is invoking the name of unscrupulous Western Zhou figure Guo Shifu 虢石父 (Guo Gu 虢鼓) here. There may be some wordplay afoot, but as discussed below, the surname is probably of greater import.

xxvii. As King Xuan points out here, the execution of the entire clan had been sanctioned as a punishment for treasonous behavior long before the Warring States. However, it was a theme that loomed particularly large in the Ming: the Ming founder ordered it several times in the process of consolidating his power, and the third Ming monarch, the Yongle emperor (r. 1402–1424) made extensive use of it to purge and dissuade dissent about the manner in which he had taken the throne from his nephew, the Jianwen emperor, in 1402. See Chan 2007. The Yongle emperor had even famously expanded the liable clansmen from the usual "nine kinships" to "ten kinships" in the case of Fang Xiaoru 方孝孺 (1357–1402), minister of the Jianwen emperor. Fang's students and peers were included as the tenth kinship. Nevertheless, there were various plots and treason attempts by enfeoffed imperial relatives throughout the dynasty, so the Yongle emperor is not the only possibility. Given that the subsequent Ming emperors were descended from the Yongle emperor and their legitimacy hence rested on the rightfulness of his inheritance of the throne, this remained a controversial and taboo topic for centuries. Meanwhile, this family's relatively rare family name Zhu 邾 is conspicuously close in both sound and form to the Zhu 朱 of the Ming ruling clan. Something else that would have underscored the connection was that there was a better-known intra-familial usurpation story with regard to King Xuan. The *Intrigues* relate that King Xuan's brother, the Lord of Jingguo 靖郭君, Tian Ying 田嬰 had in fact righteously refused a proposal to oust King Xuan while still official heir in favor of another brother, Tian Jiaoshi 田郊師. The fact that it ended in the opposite result may well have, conversely, strengthened the connection for Ming readers. For one version of the story see Crump 1996, 310.

xxviii. Historical appraisals of Lord of Mengchang vis-à-vis his large retinue were in fact much more ambivalent than Mugwort's glowing report. Sima Qian's disapproving portrayal of the figure as prideful and self-serving has been well noted (Nienhauser 1994–, vol. VII, 363–364), and at one point, a reversal of fortune resulted in the vast majority of his retainers deserting him. *Shike*, the choice of term for "retainers" throughout this episode, had taken on a meaning akin to "free-loader" or "hanger-on" by the Ming.

xxix. In this episode we glimpse the nature of *Further Sayings* as the sequel to an already established tradition. There are two levels of role reversal at play which would have been amusing for readers familiar with *Miscellaneous Stories*. First, just like the usual courtiers and subordinates, Mugwort junior is afraid to remonstrate directly and plays the master at his own game. Second, by being placed in the shoes of those monarchs who have received a similar treatment at his own hands, our protagonist is given a taste of his own medicine. See "The Humorists paradigm" in the introduction.

xxx. There are comic echoes of the proverbial story of the old man on the border losing his horse (*saiweng shima* 塞翁失馬) in this turn of events. See Liu An 1990, 853–854.

xxxi. This is one of a handful of episodes across the three compilations in which Mugwort does not appear in person. But something to note is the increased fame of Master Mugwort and his persuasive abilities in the fictional world of the Ming collections. We often seen other characters flock to him in times of need, as in *Three feet of rope* (FS:1). In the third compilation *Outer Sayings*, we even meet Mugwort impersonators (OS:10, OS:15).

xxxii. *Xianshi* 先師 (late teacher) in this case does not appear to refer to Confucius. Cycle is used for *yuan* 元 and epoch for *hui* 會.

xxxiii. More literally: "was conversant in the Five Phases," often translated as the "Five Elements" of Wood, Fire, Earth, Metal, and Water.

xxxiv. Matsueda translates *qian* 情 as *miuchi no kata* 身内の方, which is an inter-pretation along different lines.

 xxxv. More literally: "The liquid is strained from the fermented grains / And the fragrance floats above the full earthen jar. / So long as there is alcohol in there I'll be drinking it; / If there's none in there then I won't touch it. / I gulp it up like a rushing wave / And swallow it like it's leaking from a sack. / From the beginning of the night to the break of dawn / We flail about in revelry. / If when sober you drink up quickly / And when drunk there are no obscenities / And if the guests are swaying drunkenly, / Then the host will never lose heart. / Tankards by the thousand, beakers by the hundred / Is a fitting analogy. / Steady and in control of myself, / Neither fatigued nor riotous, / My effusions of jests and jibes / Have never once gotten out of order."

xxxvi. A stupid magistrate with a blind clerk is an established trope according to Matsueda (1970, 98).

xxxvii. A less likely reading is: "I was ill-disposed to punish the earlier ones. But now that they have gotten away without retribution, how else am I supposed to give vent to my resentment?"

xxxviii. Gudu ("Loner") is a two-character surname, reportedly of Xianbei 鮮卑 origin.

xxxix. This line paraphrases Mencius's persuasion of King Xuan of Qi in *Mencius*, therefore I take *shi* 十 as *qi* 其. In the *Mencius* this line is intended to remind King Xuan of the meagerness of Qi's position on the grand scale of All Under Heaven, whereas here Mugwort uses it to remind King Hui of Liang of Qi's relative might. Some intertextual humor, then.

   xl. Or perhaps, "We expect it will not come to that."

  xli. The sheer ubiquity of corruption and bribery in *Outer Sayings* distinguishes it from the previous *Mugwort*s and marks this as a particular concern of Tu Benjun, and presumably speaks to his first-hand experience of governorship in the Wanli period (1573–1620) bureaucracy. Here, we glimpse Mugwort's outrage over his acquaintance's attempt to take a cut from his connection to him, when it should have been about doing the right thing, as was made explicit by the mention of Lu Zhonglian in the original request. It is not for nothing that this is the longest episode in all three compilations: Tu Benjun has used these 650 plus characters to salvage a cathartic, perhaps even optimistic, ending out of what is a complex, clandestine predicament. One suspects that in Tu Benjun's day things did not always work out quite so neatly.

 xlii. The role of husbander is usually written *seguan* 穡官, but Tu has written it *seguan* 嗇官, literally "the stingy official."

xliii. Another possibility is that this line is voiced by the Lord of Chunshen ("I will not permit it" or "I will not confer the ox"). I have excluded that in line with the punctuation in the modern edition and in accordance with the third instance of the parallel, which looks to be in third person.

xliv. My translation lacks the strong Buddhist overtones in this line.

xlv. More literally: "Imposingly, ostentatiously, pretentiously / Cast wide that mugwort net! / When his gaze of predilection flickers about / All those around him are lit up with glory!" Although this is not a known saying, the second line, "*Ai* (*Yi*) *er ru zhang* 艾而如張," is worth revisiting. It alludes to a poem by the Tang poet Li He 李賀 (c. 790–c. 816), "Cutting Grasses for a Net" ("Yi ru zhang" 艾如張). This is a famous portrayal of the day-to-day perils faced by birds, and the most insidious on the list is a delicate, near-invisible hunting net in the State of Qi, which is cunningly disguised with mugwort leaves. Even as the farmer heeds the Wastrel's suggestion, he too falls into a Mugwort-adorned trap. Meanwhile, another pun is at play. "Ai, but like Zhang," Zhang being a very common family name, this suggests that anybody—here Doctor Wang—could be posing as our esteemed protagonist.

xlvi. More literally: "Master Mugwort asked, 'By what are you afflicted, to be so faint of breath?' The vendor replied, 'My stomach is empty while carrying my load. My hunger pangs just won't let up.' Master Mugwort asked, 'You have rice-cakes in your basket, so why don't you take one out and eat it?' The vendor replied, 'Because they've gone rancid already. Get lost and let me make my profit.'"

xlvii. This episode catapults our protagonist straight into a predicament experienced by Confucius himself. *Analects* 15.2 records that during the Master's time on the road in exile from his home state of Lu: "In Chen, they ran out of provisions. His followers had fallen ill, to the extent that they could not get up. The disciple Zilu appeared before him with a bitter expression and said, 'Must even the *junzi* (noble man) experience poverty?' The Master said, 'The *junzi* holds steadfast to his principles despite poverty. But when the *xiaoren* (petty man) experiences poverty, he resorts to debased means'" (adapted from Eno 2016). Given this famous episode, to readers of *Outer Sayings* it would have been clear that the situation Master Mugwort has been placed in is a moral litmus test.

xlviii. Alternatively, "when he opens a passage for the slow-moving it is sure to pass through," which is to say pushing through actions, laws, policies that are facing resistance or have otherwise reached a stalemate.

xlix. Another interpretation is that the Companion is not claiming to have been there, but simply pretending he had previously guessed that the Lord was a reincarnation of these figures.

l. *Shenming* 神明. My translation draws upon the sense "enlightened as if a divine being," but there is scope to interpret this line as "revered him as if a divine spirit."

li. Alternatively, *tan* 譚 could just mean "discuss."

lii. More literally: "We, the plaintiffs, are the recluses Boyi and Shuqi, / The two sons of Guzhu. / Before, because he was about to attack the Shang, / We frankly remonstrated against the Heavenly King [King Wu]. / Ashamed to eat the grain of Zhou, / We went into seclusion on Mount Shouyang, / Picking ferns and picking sow-thistle, / Constructing gardens, constructing walls. / Those roughneck rogues called Guan and Kang, / As vicious as bears, / Led the tigers and the wolves / To lay waste to our dynasty. / They invaded our territory. / They frightened our wives and children. / They attacked our elms and mulberries. / The two sides at court are both in attendance, / And the details are entrusted for consideration by the Prime Minister: / We stamped out the prodigal households, / We drove out the tyrannical ruffians, / We brought peace to the realm, / And we rebuked them to ameliorate everything far and wide. / Who is here to testify to it? Jiang Ziya, the Grand Duke's hope." Jiang Ziya was King Wen and Wu's military strategist.

liii. More literally: "Pay attention to your roles / Of a deferent host yet a proud guest / Or chopsticks will not touch lips, / Straight-backed like wood-carved figurines." Alternatively: "Drinking with a lover of pretenses / The host will be deferent and the guest proud / Chopsticks will not touch lips / As they sit straight-backed like wood-carved figurines."

liv. Or *chen* 瞋, "to cast antagonistic glances at." To read between the lines, here it would imply to make eyes at someone in a way that is intended to start a fight. *Chenpan* 嗔(瞋)盼 can also be "unclear" or "not distinguishing." An alternative interpretation is therefore that the gang, in their presumed drunkenness, mistook the incognito grandee for a lowly runner.

lv. The quoted portion leaves open the interpretation that because ruler keeps them close by, neither the woman's sleeping mat nor the man's carriage see regular use. Mugwort would in that case be referring to the fact that the Lords kept the lovelies by their sides long beyond the typical age. For the relevant story see Crump 1996, 229–230; Liu Xiang 1978, 488–490.

lvi. Mugwort here refers to the *Lost Book of Zhou* (*Yi Zhoushu* 逸周書), a compendium of historical documents on the Zhou dynasty. His quote reverses the order of the transmitted version. Here my translation, which takes *she* 舌 as *hou* 后, follows McNeal 2012, 100. Another existing interpretation is that *she* "tongue" stands for remonstrating officials. "Beautiful women bring ruin to the remonstrating officials" by pushing their own agenda with the monarch in secret. More simply, one could take *she* to indicate "speech."

In any case, the second part looks like a pun on *polao* 破老 "to enter old age," i.e., "Fine young men shall enter old age" while remaining in favor.

lvii. Reading *qihuan* 乞緩 as *qiyuan* 乞援.

lviii. *Renlun* 人倫 can also refer to an aptitude for study.

Bibliography

Editions

Chen Weili 陈维礼 and Guo Junfeng 郭俊峰, eds. 1996. In vol. 1 of *Zhongguo lidai xiaohua ji* 中国历代笑话集成 [Collection of Chinese Jokes Through the Ages]. MS: 77–91; FS: 196–207. Shidai wenyi chubanshe.

Fan Qin 范欽, prefaced. 1995. *Yanxia xiaoshuo shisan zhong* 煙霞小說一三種 [*Thirteen Tales from the Fogged-Up World*]. In *Zibu* 子部 vol. 125 of *Siku quanshu cunmu congshu* 四庫全書存目叢書, 445–705. Qilu shushe.

Su Shi 蘇軾, attrib. 1986. "Aizi zashuo" 艾子雜說 [Miscellaneous Stories of Master Mugwort]. In *Zibu* 子部 vol. 877 of *Wenyuan ge siku quanshu* 文淵閣四庫全書, 806–810. Taiwan shangwu yinshuguan.

Su Shi 蘇軾, attrib. 1960. "Dongpo jushi 'Aizi zashuo'" 東坡居士艾子雜說 [The Resident of East Slope's "Miscellaneous Stories of Master Mugwort"]. In vol. 2 of *Gushi wenfang xiaoshuo* 顧氏文房小說 [Fiction from Mr. Gu's Studio], edited by Gu Yuanqing 顧元慶, 300–308. Xinxing shuju. Also 1988. In vol. 84 of *Beijing tushuguan guji zhenben congkan* 北京圖書館古籍珍本叢刊, 316–324. Shumu wenxian chubanshe.

Tao Ting 陶珽, ed. 1995–1997. *Aizi houyu* 艾子後語 [Further Sayings of Master Mugwort]. In *Zibu* 子部 vol. 1192 of *Xuxiu siku quanshu* 續修四庫全書, 324–329. Shanghai guji chubanshe.

Tu Benjun 屠本畯, ed. 1988. *Wuzi xiece* 五子諧策 [The Jest Intrigues of the Five Masters]. In vol. 64 of *Beijing tushuguan guji zhenben congkan* 北京圖書館古籍珍本叢刊, 352–380. Shumu wenxian chubanshe.

Wang Liqi 王利器, ed. 1956. *Lidai xiaohua ji* 历代笑话集 [Jokes Through the Ages]. Shanghai gudian wenxue chubanshe.

Yang Jialuo 楊家駱, ed. 1967. *"Jiandeng xinhua" deng jiuzhong* 剪燈新話等九種 [Nine Works from "New Stories for Trimming Wicks" and Others]. Chapters 4, 5, 6 (unpaginated) for MS, FS, OS. Shijie shuju.

Translations

Dolby, William. 2005. *Chinese Humour: An Anthology*. Carreg.

Lu Yunzhong 盧允中. 1985. *100 Chinese Jokes Through the Ages*. Shangwu yinshuguan (Xianggang) youxian gongsi.

Kowallis, Jon. 1986. *Wit and Humor from Old Cathay*. Chinese Literature Press.

Matsueda Shigeo 松枝茂夫. 1970. *Rekidai shōwasen* 歷代笑話選 [Selection of Jokes Through the Ages]. Heibonsha.

Secondary Scholarship

Ahn Hei Jin 安熙珍. 2016. "*Aizi zashuo* zuozhe zhiyi" 《艾子杂说》作者质疑 [Doubts over the Authorship of *Miscellaneous Stories of Master Mugwort*]. In vol. 6 of *Zhongguo Su Shi yanjiu* 中国苏轼研究 [Chinese Studies on Su Shi], edited by Leng Chengjin 冷成金, 129–39. Xueyuan chubanshe.

Lin Shu-chen 林淑貞. 2006. *Yu zhuang yu xie: Ming-Qing xiaohuaxing yuyan lunquan* 寓莊於諧：明清笑話型寓言論詮 [Lodging the Serious in Humor: Discussions and Explications of Joke-form Fables from the Ming and Qing Dynasties]. Liren shuju.

Kong Fanli 孔凡礼. 1985. "*Aizi* shi Su Shi de zuopin" 《艾子》是苏轼的作品 [*Master Mugwort* is a Work by Su Shi]. *Wenxue yichan* 文学遗产 (3): 39–42.

Smithrosser, Elizabeth. 2021. "'Good Wood on Crowdpleasers': Humour Publications in the Ming Wanli Period." DPhil diss., University of Oxford.

Zhou Jin 周瑾. 2017. "*Aizi zashuo* yanjiu" 《艾子杂说》研究 [A Study of *Miscellaneous Stories of Master Mugwort*]. MA diss., Lanzhou University.

Zhu Jinghua 朱靖华. 1989. "Lun *Aizi zashuo* quewei Dongpo suozuo" 论《艾子杂说》确为东坡所作 [On the Certainty of *Miscellaneous Stories of Master Mugwort* Being Composed by Dongpo]. *Wenxue yichan* 文学遗产 (3): 169–181.

Works Cited

Aina the Layman. 2017. *Idle Talk Under the Bean Arbor: A Seventeenth-Century Chinese Story Collection*, edited by Robert Hegel. University of Washington Press.

Attardo, Salvatore, ed. 2014. *Encyclopedia of Humor Studies*. 2 vols. SAGE.

Baccini, Giulia. 2011a. "The Forest of Laughs (Xiaolin): Mapping the Offspring of Self-Aware Literature in Ancient China." Ph.D. diss., Ca' Foscari University of Venice.

Baccini, Giulia. 2011b. "The Xiaolin as a *Paiyou xiaoshuo*: The Origins and the Changing of Meaning of the Term *Paiyou*." In *The Yields of Transition: Literature, Art and Philosophy in Early Medieval China*, edited by Jana S. Rošker and Nataša Vampelj Suhadolnik, 157–79. Cambridge Scholars Publishing.

Baccini, Giulia. 2020. "Approaching Jokes and Jestbooks in Premodern China." In *The Palgrave Handbook of Humour, History, and Methodology*, edited by Daniel Derrin and Hannah Burrows, 201–220. Palgrave Macmillan.

Berkowitz, Alan. 2005. "Sima Qian's 'Account of the Legendary Physician Bian Que.'" In *Hawai'i Reader in Traditional Chinese Culture*, edited by Victor H. Mair, Nancy Shatzman Steinhardt, and Paul R. Goldin, 174–178. University of Hawai'i Press.

Chan, Hok-lam. 2007. "Legitimating Usurpation: Historical Revisions under the Ming Yongle Emperor." In *The Legitimation of New Orders: Case Studies in World History*, edited by Philip Yuen-sang Leung, 75–159. The Chinese University of Hong Kong Press.

Chen Jiru 陳繼儒. 1936. *Zhenzhu chuan* 珍珠船 [Boat of Precious Gems]. Shangwu yinshuguan.

Carrington, Goodrich L. and Chaoying Fang, eds. 1976. *Dictionary of Ming Biography, 1368-1644*. 2 vols. Columbia University Press.

Crump, J.I. 1996. *Chan-kuo t'se*. Center for Chinese Studies, The University of Michigan.

Crump. J.I. 1998. *Legends of the Warring States: Persuasions, Romances, and Stories from Chan-kuo ts'e*. University of Michigan Press.

Denecke, Wiebke. 2011. *The Dynamics of Masters Literature: Early Chinese Thought from Confucius to Han Feizi*. Harvard University Asia Center.

Denecke, Wiebke, Wai-Yee Li, and Xiaofei Tian, eds. 2017. *The Oxford Handbook of Classical Chinese Literature (1000 BCE–900 CE)*. Oxford University Press.

Dragon Tales: A Collection of Chinese Stories. 1988. Chinese Literature Press.

Dösch, Martin. 2013. "Ordering the World: Shao Yong and the Idea of History." *Monumenta Serica* 61: 269–285.

Du Mu 都穆. 1995–1997. *Dugong tanzuan* 都公談纂 [The Words of Mr. Du, Collated]. In Zibu 子部 vol. 1266 of *Xuxiu siku quanshu* 續修四庫全書, 641–684. Shanghai guji chubanshe.

Durrant, Stephen, Wai-yee Li and David Schaberg, trans. 2016. *Zuo Tradition / Zuozhuan: Commentary on the "Spring and Autumn Annals."* University of Washington Press.

Egan, Ronald C. 1994. *Word, Image and Deed in the Life of Su Shi*. Harvard University Asia Center.

Eno, Robert. 2016. "Mencius: An Online Teaching Translation." Version 1.0. Consulted at http://hdl.handle.net/2022/23421.

Feng Mengzhen 馮夢禎. "Feng Mengzhen Kuaixue tang ji" 馮夢禎快雪堂集 [Feng Mengzhen's Kuaixue Studio Collection], fascicle 2, 75–78. Consulted at *The Chinese Text Project*, https://ctext.org/library.pl?if=gb&file=96716& page=75&remap=gb.

Forke, Alfred. 1907. *Lun-hêng, Part I, Philosophical Essays of Wang Ch'ung*. Otto Harrassowitz.

Franke, Herbert. 1974. "Literary Parody in Traditional Chinese Literature: Descriptive Pseudo-Biographies." *Oriens Extremus* 21.1: 23–31.

Franke, Herbert, ed. 1976. *Sung Biographies*. 3 vols. Steiner.

Fraser, Chris. 2020. "School of Names." *The Stanford Encyclopedia of Philosophy* (Winter Edition), edited by Edward N. Zalta. Consulted at https://plato .stanford.edu/archives/win2020/entries/school-names/.

Graham, A.C. 1989. *Disputers of the Tao: Philosophical Argument in Ancient China*. Open Court.

Graham, A.C. 1973. *The Book of Lieh-tzu*. John Murray.

Greenbaum, Jamie. 2007. *Chen Jiru (1558–1639): The Background to, Development and Subsequent Uses of Literary Personae*. Brill.

Guben xiqu congkan bianji weiyuanhui 古本戲曲叢刊編輯委員會. 1954. In vols. 13–14 of *Guben xiqu congkan chuji* 古本戲曲叢刊初集 [Compendium of Old Plays, First Collection]. Shangwu yinshuguan. Unpaginated.

Harbsmeier, Christoph. 1998. *Science and Civilisation in China, Vol. 7, Part 1: Language and Logic.* Cambridge University Press.

Hartman, Charles. 1990. "Poetry and Politics in 1079: The Crow Terrace Poetry Case of Su Shih." *Chinese Literature, Essays, Articles, Reviews* 12: 15–44.

Hinsch, Bret. 1990. *Passions of the Cut Sleeve: The Male Homosexual Tradition in China.* University of California Press.

He, Yuming. 2013. *Home and the World: Editing the "Glorious Ming" in Woodblock-Printed Books of the Sixteenth and Seventeenth Centuries.* Harvard University Asia Center.

Hsu, Elisabeth. 2010. *Pulse Diagnosis in Early Chinese Medicine: The Telling Touch.* Cambridge University Press.

Hsu, Pi-Ching, trans. 2015. *Feng Menglong's Treasury of Laughs: A Seventeenth-century Anthology of Traditional Chinese Humour.* Brill.

Hu Yinglin 胡應麟. 1933. *Sibu zheng'e* 四部正譌 [Correcting Falsehoods in the Four Categories]. Pushe chuban jinglibu.

Hucker, Charles O. 1985. *A Dictionary of Official Titles in Imperial China.* Stanford University Press.

"Gaishi zassetsu" 艾子雜説. Definition from *Buritanika kokusai dai hyakajiten* ブリタニカ国際大百科事典 [International Encyclopaedia Britannica], Britannica Japan Co., consulted at Kotobank コトバンク, https://kotobank.jp/word/ 艾子雜説-42448.

Kroll, Paul W. 2017. *A Student's Dictionary of Classical and Medieval Chinese: Revised Edition.* Brill.

Kubo, Tsugunari and Akira Yuyama. 2007. "The Lotus Sutra." Numata Center for Buddhist Translation and Research. Consulted at https://www.bdk.or.jp/ document/dgtl-dl/dBET_T0262_LotusSutra_2007.pdf.

Kutcher, Norman A. 2018. *Eunuch and Emperor in the Great Age of Qing Rule.* University of California Press.

Li, Jingrong. 2022. "The Governance of New Territories During the Qin Unification." *T'oung Pao* 108.1–2: 1–35.

Li, Wai-yee. 2013. "Riddles, Concealment, and Rhetoric in Early China." In *Facing the Monarch: Modes of Advice in the Early Chinese Court*, edited by Garret P. S. Olberding, 100–132. Harvard University Asia Center.

Li Ye 李冶 [also Li Zhi 李治]. 1935. *Jingzhai gujin tou fu shiyi* 敬齋古今黈附拾遺 [Jingzhai's Notes on Past and Present with Appended Information]. Shangwu yinshuguan.

Liu An 劉安, ed., et al. 1990. *Huainanzi yizhu* 淮南子译注 [The *Huainanzi*, Translated and Annotated]. Jilin wenshi chubanshe.

Liu Shangrong 刘尚荣. 1988. *Su Shi zhuzuo banben luncong* 苏轼著作版本论丛 [Collection of Essays on Editions of Works by Su Shi]. Bashu shushe.

Liu Xiang 劉向, ed. 1978. *Zhanguo ce* 戰國策 [Intrigues of the Warring States]. 3 vols. Shanghai guji chubanshe.

Lin Yutang. 1947. *The Gay Genius: The Life and Times of Su Tungpo*. The John Day Co.

Liu Cifu 劉慈孚. 1966. *Simingren jian* 四明人鑑 [A Mirror of People in Siming]. In vol 6.5 of *Siming congshu* 四明叢書, edited by Chang Chi-yun 張其昀, 327–422. Guofang yanjiuyuan and Zhonghua dadian bianyinhui.

Loewe, Michael and Edward L. Shaughnessy, eds. 1999. *The Cambridge History of Ancient China: From the Origins of Civilization to 221 B.C.*. Cambridge University Press.

Lu Cai 陸采. 1995–1997. *Tianchi shanren xiaogao wuzhong* 天池山人小稿五種 [Five Little Drafts by the Mountain-man of the Heavenly Pool]. In Jibu 集部 vol. 1354 of *Xuxiu siku quanshu* 續修四庫全書, 1–334. Shanghai guji chubanshe.

Lu Can 陸粲. 1974. *Lu Ziyu ji* 陸子餘集 [*The Lu Ziyu Collection*]. Taiwan shangwu yinshuguan.

Mai, Huijun. 2020. "The Double Life of the Scallop: Anthropomorphic Biography, 'Pulu,' and the Northern Song Discourse on Things." *Journal of Song-Yuan Studies* 49: 149–205.

Mao Jin 毛晉. 1988. *Shanju xiaowan* 山居小玩 [Little Amusements for Mountain Living]. In vol. 78 of *Beijing tushuguan guji zhenben congkan* 北京圖書館古籍珍本叢刊, 431–558. Shumu wenxian chubanshe.

Mingren zhuanji ziliao suoyin 明人傳記資料索引 [Index of Biographical Materials on Ming Figures]. 1978. Guoli zhongyang tushuguan.

Miyazaki Ichisada. 1967. "The Reforms of Wang An-shih." In *Wang An-Shih, Practical Reformer?: Problems in Asian Civilizations*, edited by John Meskill, 82–90. D. C. Heath and Company.

McNeal, Robin. 2012. *Conquer and Govern: Early Chinese Military Texts from the Yi Zhou shu*. University of Hawai'i Press.

Nienhauser, Jr., William H., ed. 1994–. *The Grand Scribe's Records*. Indiana University Press with Nanjing University Press. References are to updated and revised versions as of April 2022, otherwise the originals.

Pines, Yuri. 2009. *Envisioning Eternal Empire: Chinese Political Thought of the Warring States Era*. University of Hawai'i Press.

Pinshiwen 品诗文. 2019. "Su Shi 'Qinda wushi sheng churu'" 苏轼《禽大无事省出入》 [Su Shi's "Old Qin should go out less given that he has nothing to do"]. *Pinshiwen* 品诗文 (Feb 16). Consulted at https://www.pinshiwen.com/wenfu/sanwen/201902162818.html.

Pokora, Timoteus. 1972. "The Etymology of *ku-chi* (or *hua-chi*)." *Zeitschrift der Deutschen Morgenländischen Gesellschaft* 122: 149–72.

Porter, Deborah Lynn. 1996. *From Deluge to Discourse: Myth, History, and the Generation of Chinese Fiction*. SUNY Press.

Rao, Xiao. 2022. "Humor under the Guise of Chan: Stories of Su Shi and Encounter Dialogues." *Journal of the American Oriental Society* 142.2: 311–333.

Rea, Christopher. 2015. *The Age of Irreverence: A New History of Laughter in China*. University of California Press.

Ridgway, Benjamin and Kathleen Tomlonovic. 2017. "Su Shi (Su Dongpo)." *Oxford Bibliographies*. Consulted at DOI: 10.1093/OBO/9780199920082-0142.

Sima Qian. 1973. *Shiji* 史記 [Records of the Historian]. 6 vols. Zhonghua shuju.

Shen Yiguan 沈一貫. 1995–1997. *Huiming wenji* 喙鳴文集 [Collected Writings from the Chirpings of All Beaks]. In Jibu 集部 vol. 1357 of *Xuxiu siku quanshu* 續修四庫全書, 107–517. Shanghai guji chubanshe.

Smithrosser, Elizabeth. 2016. "Becoming the 'Bull-Headed Premier': On the Literary Portrayals of Wang Anshi from the Southern Song to Ming (1127-1644)." M.St. diss., University of Oxford.

Smithrosser, Elizabeth. 2024. "*The Biography of Ye Jia* (A Tea-Leaf Tale)." *Renditions: A Chinese-English Translation Magazine*.

Smithrosser, Elizabeth. 2022. "Un-learning the *Stratagems*: Qing Pedagogical Efforts against Poisonous Warring States Legacies." *Sulla Via del Catai* Special Issue: Virtuous Youngsters and Where to Find Them: Educational Pathways and Representations of Young People in the Chinese Pedagogical and Literary Traditions, 69–87. Extended version accessible at: https://www.martinomartinicenter.org/uploads/2/2/8/5/22856686/25_smithrosser_43-52.pdf.

Standaert, Nicolas. 2016. *The Intercultural Weaving of Historical Texts: Chinese and European Stories about Emperor Ku and His Concubines*. Brill.

Tan Qixiang 譚其驤. 1982. *Zhongguo lishi dituji* 中国历史地图集 [Collection of Maps of Historical China], vol. 1. Ditu chubanshe.

Tu Benjun 屠本畯. 1939. *Minzhong haicuo shu* 閩中海錯疏 [Explanatory Notes on the Seafood Varieties along the Southeastern Coast]. Shangwu yinshuguan. Also 1986. In Shibu 史部 vol. 590 of *Wenyuan ge siku quanshu* 文淵閣四庫全書, 499–525. Taiwan shangwu yinshuguan.

Tu Benjun 屠本畯, ed. 1988. *Shanlin jingji ji* 山林經濟籍 [The Mountain-Forest Administrator's Companion]. In vol. 64 of *Beijing tushuguan guji zhenben congkan* 北京圖書館古籍珍本叢刊, 352–80. Shumu wenxian chubanshe.

Tu Long 屠隆. 2012. *Tu Long ji* 屠隆集 [The Tu Long Collection]. 12 vols., edited by Wang Chaohong 王超宏. Zhejiang guji chubanshe.

Tsai, Shih-shan Henry. 1996. *The Eunuchs in the Ming Dynasty*. SUNY Press.

Tsien, Tsuen-hsuin. 1993. "Chan kuo ts'e." In *Early Chinese Texts: A Bibliographical Guide*, edited by Michael Loewe, 1–11. Society for the Study of Early China and the Institute of East Asian Studies.

Wang, Jing, trans. 2020. "The Tale of Wushuang the Peerless." In *Anthology of Tang and Song Tales: The* Tang Song chuanqi ji *of Lu Xun*, edited by Victor Mair and Zhenjun Zhang, 358–373. World Scientific.

Wang, Xing. 2020. *Physiognomy in Ming China: Fortune and the Body*. Brill.

Wilkinson, Endymion. 2022. *Chinese History: A New Manual*. 2 vols. Harvard University Asia Center.

Weingarten, Oliver. 2017. "Chunyu Kun: Motifs, Narratives, and Personas in Early Chinese Anecdotal Literature." *Journal of the Royal Asiatic Society* 27.3: 501–521.

Werner, E.T.C. 1961. *A Dictionary of Chinese Mythology*. The Julian Press.

Wu Renjie 吳仁傑 and Tu Benjun 屠本畯. 1995. *Lisao caomu shu bu* 離騷草木疏補 [Explanatory Notes on the Vegetation in Lisao, Supplemented]. In Jibu 集部 vol. 1 of *Siku quanshu cunmu congshu* 四庫全書存目叢書. Qilu shushe.

Wu Xiangxiang 吳相湘, series ed. 1966. *Mingchao kaiguo wenxian* 明朝開國文獻 [Documents on the Founding of the Ming Dynasty]. Taiwan xuesheng shuju.

Xu, Weihe. 2011. "The Classical Confucian Concepts of Human Emotion and Proper Humour." In *Humour in Chinese Life and Letters: Classical and Traditional Approaches*, edited by Jocelyn Chey and Jessica Milner Davies, 49–72. Hong Kong University Press.

Yang Bojun 杨伯峻. 1979. *Liezi jishi* 列子集释 [Collected Commentaries on the *Liezi*]. Zhonghua shuju.

Yang Kuan 楊寬. 1955. *Zhanguo shi* 戰國史 [History of the Warring States]. Shanghai renmin chubanshe.

Yang Jingzhao 杨敬昭 and Li Shian 李仕安, eds. 1982. *Hanfeizi jiaozhu* 韩非子校注 [The *Hanfeizi*, Corrected and Annotated]. Jiangsu renmin chubanshe.

Yang, Zhiyi. 2014. "Sū Shì (1037–1101)." In *Berkshire Dictionary of Chinese Biography*. Berkshire Publishing.

Yimen Junyu 夷門君玉. 2013. *Guolao tanyuan* 國老談苑 [Garden of Discussions by State Elders]. In vol. 2.2 of *Quan Song biji* 全宋筆記. Daxiang chubanshe.

Ziporyn, Brook. 2009. *Zhuangzi: The Essential Writings: With Selections from Traditional Commentaries*. Hackett Publishing.

Ziporyn, Brook. 2020. *Zhuangzi: The Complete Writings*. Hackett Publishing.

Zhang Shuying 張樹英, ed. 2000. *Mingzhu ji Nanxixiang ji* 明珠記 南西廂記 [Record of the Bright Pearl and Record of the Southwestern Chamber]. Zhonghua shuju.